ENCOUNTERS
with NATURE SPIRITS

FINDHORN CLASSICS

ENCOUNTERS
with NATURE SPIRITS

Co-creating with the Elemental Kingdom

R. OGILVIE CROMBIE

FINDHORN PRESS

Findhorn Press
One Park Street
Rochester, Vermont 05767
www.findhornpress.com

Findhorn Press is a division of Inner Traditions International

Copyright © 2009, 2018 by Findhorn Foundation et al

Please refer to 'Sources and Acknowledgments' for additional copyright information.

Originally published in 2009 in two editions under the titles:
– *The Gentleman and the Faun: Encounters with Pan and the Elemental Kingdom* (Findhorn Press, UK edition)
– *Meeting Fairies: My Remarkable Encounters with Nature Spirit*s (Allen & Unwin, international edition)

A CIP record for this title is available from the Library of Congress

ISBN 978-1-62055-837-9 (print)
ISBN 978-1-62055-895-9 (ebook)

Printed and bound in the United States

10 9 8 7 6 5 4 3 2

Illustrations by Elise Hurst
Photograph of ROC on p. v courtesy of Findhorn Foundation
Text design and layout by Christabella Designs
This book was typeset in Old Claude and Goudy Oldstyle with P22 Stanyan used as a display typeface.

Ogilvie, the Merlin figure, surely to us is Gandalf,
the White Magician.

SIR GEORGE TREVELYAN

CONTENTS

Robert Ogilvie Crombie, or Roc, was a loving and gentle man, a wondrous storyteller, a musician, an actor, and an embodiment of the best of Scottish charm. He was the wise old man, the grandfatherly figure children adore, and the magician who guides heroes and heroines on their paths of accomplishment. He was a man of culture who had one foot in this world and one foot in the worlds of spirit and mystery.

There was a great deal to admire about Roc. He was a self-taught mythologist, psychologist, historian and esotericist, though his early training had been in science. Though quiet and reserved, he was still a pleasure to be with. He had a delightful, even impish, sense of humour matched by a twinkle in his eyes that was rarely absent.

DAVID SPANGLER

PROLOGUE

How it all began

•

MIKE SCOTT, MUSICIAN, WRITER AND ARCHIVIST

R Ogilvie Crombie was an Edinburgh man, born in that most gracious of cities into an artistic, well-to-do family in the spring of 1899. As a child he played piano, excelled at maths and science, and read the books on parapsychology he found in his father's library, an interest that developed into teenage experiments in telepathy and automatic writing. But though young Ogilvie—the 'R' stood for Robert but his friends called him by his middle name—enjoyed rambling over the Braid Hills that lay south of the family home, he was not a hardy lad. When he was nine it was discovered his heart had a leaking mitral valve, a condition for which in those days there was no treatment.

Thus, at a young age, the major strands of Ogilvie's life were established: the arts and sciences, a fragile heart and an interest in the unseen.

On leaving school in 1915 he joined the Marconi radio company as a trainee, then served as a radio operator in the Merchant Navy during the latter part of the First World War. At war's end he went to Edinburgh University where he studied physics, chemistry and mathematics, but after three years Ogilvie's studies were curtailed by illness. When he was thirty-three, he suffered a serious heart attack and was told by his doctor to 'consider himself retired'. Prevented from working, Ogilvie was free to dedicate himself to his interests, and immersed himself in the cultural life of Edinburgh. He was a founding member of the famous Scottish theatre group The Makars, and in the 1930s became, as one newspaper said, 'a well-known personality in Edinburgh dramatic circles'. He also wrote and directed plays and in later years regularly appeared on Scottish television playing small character parts—a judge here, a professor there. His credits included popular series such as *Dr Finlay's Casebook*, and he appeared as an extra in the Peter Sellers movie *The Battle of the Sexes*, where he can be briefly glimpsed strolling up Edinburgh's Royal Mile.

Ogilvie was that rare kind of man who is interested in everything. He performed piano recitals, led a choir, edited poetry journals and formed a philosophical society. In his rich Edinburgh brogue he gave talks on classical music and the appreciation of paintings. He kept abreast of developments in science and medicine, wrote letters to newspapers, and followed all of the arts with a sharp eye. Yet running ever parallel with these pursuits, and as private as his enjoyment of acting was public, was Ogilvie's interest in the deeper mysteries of life.

There is no doubt that Ogilvie was an initiate of an ancient and veiled spiritual tradition. His lectures and writings of the 1960s and 70s, which comprise the major part of this book, intermingled with recollections by others who were there, bear the hallmarks of the adept: authority, humility, curiosity, encyclopaedic yet integrated knowledge, and the tantalising sense of greater wisdom held perpetually in reserve behind a nuanced boundary of well-weighed words. It is not known to which school or system he belonged, nor is it important. Ogilvie never revealed his spiritual lineage, but it's clear he had a profound understanding not only of what used to be called 'the occult' but of all the world's major religions, and many of its more obscure ones.

This sheathed mastery was matched by Ogilvie's profound understanding of nature, which sprang from his scientific interests and his lifelong love of hill walks, fresh air and bathing in the sea. Ogilvie's empathy with the natural world deepened significantly during his ten-year experience of living in an isolated rural cottage. Ordered out of Edinburgh by his doctor at the outbreak of the Second World War, lest his fragile health be broken in the event of German bombings, Ogilvie lived an ascetic life in Cowford Cottage, Perthshire. There was no electricity and he fetched his water from a nearby spring, but the absence of modern comforts and the immanent presence of nature acted powerfully upon the curious and sensitive Ogilvie, who gradually became more and more subtly aware of the natural world around him. By oil lamp and candle he studied Jung and Plato, and among the multitude of books he read was Paramahansa Yogananda's then newly published *Autobiography of a Yogi*. And though he kept in touch with the distant fortunes of humanity by newspapers and radio, Ogilvie existed for those ten years not unlike a medieval hermit: removed from the tides of men and alert to the deeper rhythms of the world.

He returned to Edinburgh in 1949 and lived in a first-floor flat on Albany Street, close to the city centre, where he would stay until his death in 1975. Most of the experiences recounted in this book occurred during the last decade of his life, and it was during this period that Ogilvie made the only public displays of his interest in occult matters. These took the form of lectures and were spurred in part by his friendship with a former RAF officer named Peter Caddy and his subsequent involvement in the spiritual community of which Caddy was co-founder, the Findhorn Foundation in northeast Scotland.

Though today world-renowned and numbering hundreds of members, at the time Ogilvie met Caddy the community at Findhorn comprised five adults whose little-known work was centred around two mystical yet practical activities. Peter, his wife Eileen and their friend Dorothy Maclean had been trained in a variety of spiritual disciplines, and Eileen and Dorothy had each learned to contact personal inner sources of guidance in meditation. The experience of an 'inner guiding voice' is common to all spiritual traditions, and was termed by Eileen '*the still small voice within*'. Following the directions Eileen received inwardly, Peter had unconventionally but successfully managed a large Scottish hotel for several years, and the group was now establishing their fledgling community the same way.

In 1963 their work had expanded into a dynamic cooperation with nature when Dorothy discovered, also in meditation, that like a human radio receiver she could tune into and contact the overlighting angelic spirits of plants, subtle intelligences she called 'devas'. Short of cash and struggling to grow food in their meagre garden, Peter persuaded a bemused Dorothy to ask the devas for planting advice. And the devas responded. Soon, amazingly, the Findhorn group was receiving precise gardening instructions from the inner intelligences of nature, resulting, by the mid 60s, in an astonishingly abundant garden grown in the unlikely sandy soil of a wind-lashed caravan park. This miraculous 'Findhorn garden' had profound implications not only spiritually, but for ecology, land reclamation and food creation; if humanity and nature could cooperate like this around the world, what might be achieved? The small group wasn't yet ready to reveal their secret for fear of disbelief and ridicule; nevertheless, the garden became famous when a parade of horticultural experts, first local then national, visited and pronounced themselves stunned and mystified.

This was the kind of intriguing development, blending science, nature and the unseen, that was sure to grip the ever-curious Ogilvie's attention. And so it did; Ogilvie soon became a regular and much-loved visitor to the community, where he was always known by the acronym 'Roc'. In fact, he became the community's mentor, Peter Caddy's first port of call whenever any esoteric advice was required, and is now remembered as one of its major early figures, along with the three founders and David Spangler.

But most importantly, beyond mentorship, Ogilvie brought to Findhorn a third connection with the subtler worlds. For in early 1966, even before he had an opportunity to see the miracle garden for himself, Ogilvie made his own startling contact with the inner spirits of nature. It happened on a March day in an Edinburgh park, and nothing would ever be the same again.

AFTERNOON WITH A FAUN
·

ROC

Over forty years ago something rather special happened.
R. Ogilvie Crombie, or Roc as he was often known, visited
the Royal Botanic Garden in Edinburgh, not far from his
flat. It was here, in one of his favourite places, that he was to
have an experience that proved life-changing.

It was a glorious day and I went to the Garden in the afternoon. I wandered about for a while enjoying the beauty and peace of the rock garden and other favourite spots. Eventually I began walking along a path skirting the north side of Inverleith House, which is situated on rising ground in the centre of the Garden and houses Edinburgh's Modern Art Gallery.

Leaving the path I crossed an expanse of grass, dotted with trees and bushes, to a seat under a tall beech tree. When I sat down I leant my shoulders and the back of my head against the tree. I became, in some way, identified with this tree, became aware of the movement of the sap in the trunk and even of the infinitely slow growth of the roots. There was a decided heightening of awareness and a sense of expectation. I felt completely awake and full of energy. There was a tension in the air, almost as if the air itself were beginning to shimmer. I sat there in utter contentment.

Suddenly I saw a figure dancing round a tree about twenty yards away from me—a beautiful little figure about three feet tall. I saw with astonishment that it was a faun, the Greek mythological being, half human, half animal. He had a pointed chin and ears and two little horns on his forehead. His shaggy legs ended in cloven hooves and his skin was honey-coloured. I looked at him in amazement, and even did the obvious: I pinched myself. I was awake.

I wondered for a moment if perhaps he was a boy made up for a school show. Yet he could not be—something about him was decidedly not human. Was he an hallucination? There were one or two other people walking about in the Garden. I looked at them and then back at this beautiful little being. He was still there and seemed to be as solid and real as they were. I tried hard to analyse this experience and explain him away.

Suddenly I was brought up sharp—what was I trying to do? Here was a strange and wonderful experience. Why should I not accept it, see what happened and analyse it later? I watched the little being with delight as he circled around another tree. He danced over to where I was sitting, stood looking at me for a moment and then sat cross-legged in front of me. I looked at him. He was very real. I bent forward and said: 'Hallo.'

He leapt to his feet, startled, and stared at me. 'Can you see me?'

'Yes.'

'I don't believe it,' he said. 'Humans can't see us.'

'Oh, yes,' I assured him. 'Some of us can.'

'What am I like?' he asked.

I described him as I saw him. Still looking bewildered, he began to dance around in small circles. 'What am I doing?'

I told him. He stopped dancing and said, 'You must be seeing me.'

He danced across to the seat beside me, sat down and, turning towards me, looked up and said: 'Why are human beings so stupid?'

In some ways I may be over-personalising this being. I realise I was not seeing him with my physical sight, though when I closed my eyes he was not there. And the communication between us was, no doubt, taking place on a mental or telepathic level by means of thought transference, probably in the form of images and symbols projected into my unconscious mind and translated into words by my consciousness. I cannot be certain as to whether I was speaking to him mentally or aloud, however I have to report our exchanges in the form of dialogue, since that is what I heard in my head. I am aware that in a case like this there is always the possibility of colouration from my own mind.

However, applying my training as a scientist in objective observation and analysis, I do try to report experiments and experiences as accurately as possible.

To return to this question of why human beings are so stupid, I asked him, 'In what way stupid?'

'In many ways.' He wanted to know what were the strange skins or coverings they had, some of which could be taken off? Why did they not go about in the natural state as he did?

I told him the skins were called clothes and that we wore them for protection and for warmth and because it was not considered right to be without them. This latter he could not understand, so I did not pursue the subject. We talked about houses, and motor cars which seemed to him to be boxes on wheels in which human beings dashed about, sometimes bumping into each other. 'Was it a game?' he wanted to know.

He told me he lived in the Garden. This was a partial truth, as he was an inhabitant of another plane as well. His work was to help the growth of trees. He also told me that many of the nature spirits have lost interest in the human race, since they have been made to feel that they are neither believed in nor wanted.

'If you humans think you can get along without us, just try!'

'Some of us do believe in you and want your help. I do, for one.'

The wonderful thing about this meeting was the sense of companionship. I felt an amazing harmony with this wonderful little being sitting beside me. A communication was taking place between us that did not need to be put in words. We sat for some time without speaking. Eventually I rose and said I must return home.

'Call me when you return here and I will come to you,' he said. He told me his name was Kurmos. I asked him if he could visit me.

'Yes, if you invite me,' he replied.

'I do. I shall be delighted if you will come and visit me.'

'You do believe in me?'

'Yes, of course I do.'

'And you like us?' asked Kurmos.

'Yes, I have much affection for the nature spirits.' This was true from childhood, though he was the first one I had actually seen.

'Then I'll come now.'

We walked through the west gate out of the Garden and through the streets of Edinburgh back to my flat. I was amused to think of the sensation it might have caused had this strange, delightful little faun been as visible to the passers-by as he was to me.

We entered my flat. I have a fairly large collection of books and my two main rooms are lined with bookshelves. Kurmos showed great interest. What were they and why did I have so many? I explained to him that they contained facts, ideas, speculations and theories, accounts of past events, stories invented by the writers and so on, all of which were written down, put into print and made up into books which could be read by others.

His comment was: 'Why? You can get all the knowledge you want by simply wanting it.'

I told him human beings could not do that very wonderful thing—at least not yet. We had to be content to get our facts and knowledge from other people or books.

Again we sat for some time in silence and contented harmony. It was a simple awareness of each other, something like that between a human being and a much-loved animal, an awareness that is only felt between humans when there is great harmony. It was very pleasant. This type of harmony is universal amongst the nature spirits. Dissension and hatred are almost unknown.

Then he got up; it was time for him to return to the Garden. The door of the room was open, and he walked into the hall. I followed him and, probably because he looked so solid and real, I opened the door onto the landing. He passed me and ran lightly down the stairs. As he reached the bottom step, he faded out.

This was an astonishing experience, one I am certain I could not have imagined. And why did he appear to me as a faun? That puzzled me. I had read no Greek mythology for years.

Several times after that he appeared beside me when I went to the Garden and called to him. I did not want to ask him questions; the wonderful companionship and harmony were enough, though I knew that here was infinite, mature wisdom—combined with the naiveté of a child. I intuitively felt that what was right for me to know regarding him would be given at the appropriate time.

I did not know then that these meetings with Kurmos were leading me to something even more unusual which was to take place over a month later, at the end of April.

AN EVENING ENCOUNTER

·

ROC

One evening I had been visiting friends who lived on the south side of Edinburgh. It was eleven o'clock and I was walking home. I had reached the Mound, which is the street joining the old and new towns. It runs from High Street to the middle of Princes Street in a double curve. On the left side is the castle perched on its rock above the railway and West Princes Street Gardens. On the right, at the foot of the street, are two Greek-like buildings, the Royal Scottish Academy facing Princes Street and, immediately behind it, the National Gallery.

It was a beautiful night. There were few people about, and I thought how peaceful the city was at that moment. Suddenly, as I turned the corner onto the last part of the street which runs down the side of the National Gallery, I stepped into an extraordinary atmosphere. I had never before encountered anything quite like it. While it is difficult to describe, I might say it was as if I had no clothes on and was walking through a medium denser than air but not as dense as water. I could feel it against my body. It produced a sensation of warmth and tingling like a mixture of pins and needles and an electric shock, and there was a suggestion of cobwebs brushing against my skin. This was accompanied by a heightened awareness and the same feeling of expectation I had had in the Garden before meeting Kurmos.

Then I realised that I was not alone. A figure—taller than myself—was walking beside me. It was a faun, radiating a tremendous power. I glanced at him. Surely this was not my little faun grown up suddenly?

We walked on. He turned his head and looked at me. 'Well, aren't you afraid of me?'

'No.'

'Why not? All human beings are afraid of me.'

'I feel no evil in your presence. I see no reason why you should want to harm me. I do not feel afraid.'

'Do you know who I am?'

I did at that moment. 'You are the great god Pan.'

'Then you ought to be afraid. Your word "panic" comes from the fear my presence causes,' said Pan.

'Not always. I am not afraid.'

'Can you give me a reason?' pressed Pan.

'It may be because of my affinity with your subjects, the earth spirits and woodland creatures.'

'You believe in my subjects?'

'Yes.'

'Do you love my subjects?' Pan asked.

'Yes, I do.'

'In that case, do you love me?' questioned Pan.

'Why not?'

'Do you love me?' pressed Pan.

'Yes.'

He looked at me with a strange smile and a glint in his deep, mysterious brown eyes. 'You know, of course, that I'm the devil? You have just said you love the devil.'

'No, you are not the devil. You are the god of the woodlands and the countryside. There is no evil in you. You are Pan.'

'Did the early Christian church not take me as a model for the devil? Look at my cloven hooves, my shaggy legs and the horns on my forehead.'

'The church turned all pagan gods and spirits into devils, fiends and imps.'

'Was the church wrong then?'

'The church did it with the best intentions from its own point of view. But it was wrong. The ancient gods are not necessarily devils.'

We crossed Princes Street and turned right towards South St David Street. He turned to me: 'What do I smell like?'

Since he had joined me I had been aware of a wonderful scent of pine woods, of damp leaves, of

ROC MEETS KURMOS IN THE BOTANIC GARDEN

newly turned earth and of woodland flowers. I told him this.

'Don't I smell rank like a goat?' asked Pan.

'No, you don't. There is a faint, musk-like smell, like the fur of a healthy cat. It is pleasant—almost like incense. Are you still claiming to be the devil?'

'I have to find out what you think of me. It's important.'

'Why?'

'For a reason,' said Pan.

'Won't you tell me what it is?'

'Not now. It will become apparent in time.'

We walked on. Pan was walking very close to me. 'You don't mind me walking beside you?'

'Not in the least.'

He put his arm around my shoulder. I felt the actual physical contact. 'You don't mind if I touch you?'

'No.'

'You really feel no repulsion or fear?'

'None.'

'Excellent.'

I could not think why he was making this determined effort to produce a sign of fear. I am not claiming to be a brave man; there are many things that would scare me out of my life. But, for some reason or other, I felt no fear of this being. Awe, because of his power, but not fear—only love.

We turned into Queen Street and I asked him where his panpipes were. He smiled at the question: 'I do have them, you know.' And there he was, holding them in his hands. He began to play a curious melody. I had heard it in woods before and I have often heard it since, but it is so elusive that I have always been unable to remember it afterwards.

When we reached the downstairs front door of my flat he disappeared, but when I came into the house I had a strong feeling that he was there though I could not see him.

I had no idea why this strange encounter had happened, or why this being had chosen to show himself to me. It looked as if the meeting with the little faun in the Botanic Garden had been a preliminary step in bringing it about, and I was feeling reasonably certain that neither of these beings was imaginary. I wondered what was going to happen next.

MEETING PAN ON IONA

·

ROC

The next significant meeting was in early May on Iona, a tiny island of the Inner Hebrides which is considered to be an ancient centre of spiritual power. Peter Caddy and I were standing in the Hermit's Cell, a ring of stones which is all that is left of the place where Saint Columba used to go in retreat. It is about halfway across the island, almost on a level with Iona Abbey.

In front of us was a gentle grassy slope, and I became aware of a large figure lying in the ground there. I could see him through the grass. It appeared to be a monk in a brown habit with the hood pulled over his head so that his features were concealed. His feet were towards me.

As I watched, he raised his hands and rolled back the hood. It was Pan. He rose up out of the ground and stood facing us, an immense figure at least twenty-five feet tall. As he did so, the habit fell away. He was smiling and said: 'I am the servant of Almighty God, and I and my subjects are willing to come to the aid of mankind, in spite of the way it has treated us and abused nature, if it affirms belief in us and asks for our help.'

Through this and other encounters with Pan, I would come to a greater understanding of why Pan and the nature spirits were choosing to communicate with me. Here was a step towards the reconciliation of Pan and the world of the nature spirits with humanity. Because I had been able to respond to him without fear, Pan could communicate with me and use me as a mediator between humanity and nature. This does not make me important in myself—I am simply a channel for his work.

Vital to this reconciliation is the recognition of Pan's true nature. He is a great being, the god of the whole elemental kingdom as well as of the animal, vegetable and mineral kingdoms. People may feel uneasy in his presence because of the awe he inspires, but there ought to be no fear.

'All human beings are afraid of me,' he had said at our first meeting, not as a threat but with sadness. 'Did the early Christian church not take me as a model for the devil?' That is why Pan is feared—because of the image projected onto him. This stigma must be lifted in order to re-establish the true link between humanity and nature.

Pan has said to me he would prefer not to be represented in any material form at all. Yet, if he must be, he insists on being accepted, in our culture, as the Greek myth depicts him, half human, half animal. There is a fitness about it in its symbolism. The human upper half represents intellect, united with a powerful, mysterious, deep energy represented by the animal lower half—an energy not yet revealed in humanity.

It is important to consider Pan and the nature spirits in their own right when they take on these human-like forms and not compare them with our own perception of human beauty. Some people assume that Pan must be ugly. This is far from the case. In his own right he is one of the most beautiful beings I have ever seen. Only the horns on the forehead, the cloven hooves and the fine silky hair on the legs suggest the animal part. The legs themselves are human, not animal.

It is very important to realise that though Pan can appear in such a form, he is not a being restricted to one place. The word 'pan' also means 'all', 'everywhere'. Pan is a universal energy, a cosmic energy, which is constantly found throughout the whole of nature. He could appear personified in many different places at the same time and should never be thought of as restricted to a corner of the garden or sitting on a hilltop beside a gorse bush.

It may be helpful to consider why Pan and the nature spirits assume such forms. Their primary state is what may be termed a 'light body'. It is a whirl or vortex of energy in constant motion. Nebulous like a fine mist, it glows with coloured light, sometimes one single colour, sometimes two or more which do not mix but remain separate like the colours of a rainbow. It frequently changes colour and is often covered with a multitude of fine curved lines, which appear to flow like liquid in a pipe, forming continually changing patterns of incredible beauty.

These light bodies differ from each other in size and brilliancy, varying from pastel shades to strong, bright colours. All are beautiful, pure and luminous, glowing with inner radiance. They may be regarded as whirls of energy, but energy with intelligence. It is possible to see and to communicate with these light bodies.

However, the elementals or nature spirits cannot carry out their work with plants in these pure bodies. In this work they use the energies channelled to them by the devas to build up an 'etheric body' or 'etheric counterpart' for each plant, according to its archetypal pattern. The plant grows and develops within this counterpart. In order to fulfil their task, the nature spirits too must take on an etheric body.

In esoteric knowledge, the etheric plane is made up of a fine energy substance from which is created the mould for every form we see manifest on the physical plane. Each material form has an etheric counterpart. That such a thing exists at all will be questioned by many people. At the moment it cannot be scientifically proven, though no doubt this will be possible in the future. We do know ourselves to be far more than just our physical bodies.

According to esoterics, we have an etheric body, as well as other, higher bodies. We are incarnate spirit. So, too, do plants have at least etheric bodies, if not higher ones as well. This is why humanity must be careful when it interferes with the natural growth of plants. In trying to alter the form through artificial means, often using force, humanity can depart from the archetypal design. Apart from the fear and pain produced in the plant, this can bring about lack of alignment with the esoteric counterpart, causing further discomfort and distress.

Rather than using force to bring about changes in plants, it would be much better if we would ask the nature spirits to bring them about by modifying the etheric counterpart. This they will do if they are convinced that the change is reasonable and a help to mankind, not simply for expediency. At the moment, they are limited in their actions by the general human disbelief in their power and even in their existence.

What of the etheric bodies of the nature spirits themselves? In myths, legends and fairytales, humanity has depicted a vast gallery of what it has referred to as 'supernatural' beings ('paraphysical' would be a more accurate word to describe them). To what extent the etheric forms of these beings were the product of humanity's own creative imagination or the result of inspiration from an outside source is difficult to determine. Suffice it to say there exists what one might call a vast reservoir of 'thought forms' produced by the existence and persistence of these tales. Often thought about and talked about, these forms have been preserved both orally and in print. Thus, an elemental entity wishing to assume a body can 'put on' any of these thought forms and appear personified as that particular being—Greek or Norse god, elf, gnome, faun, fairy and so on. In myths and legends these paraphysical beings have been depicted in a human form and as behaving in a human manner. Of course, they are essentially formless and only adopt a form and its characteristic behaviour when needed.

AN ENCHANTED MOMENT

·

ROC

*Once established, the relationship Roc developed with Pan
was ongoing, and from each encounter Roc gained deeper
understanding of his form and nature. In September 1966
Roc attended a weekend course at Attingham Park in
Shropshire, a pioneering adult education college. Established
in 1947, Attingham Park was run by Sir George Trevelyan
with a spiritual vision of bringing people together, giving them
a sense of meaning in life and providing them with enthusiasm
and tools for self-development through cultivating new skills
and wider capacities. The classes and workshops covered a*

wide array of topics, among them increasingly spiritual ones that proved to be very popular. Here Roc later on also gave lectures on the elemental world and perception.

Before leaving on Monday morning, I was prompted to go to an area known as the Mile Walk on Attingham's extensive and beautiful grounds.

I followed the path until I came to the Rhododendron Walk, which is considered by some to be a place of great spiritual power. At its entrance is a huge cedar tree with a bench beneath it. I sat there for some time, enjoying the beauty of the place, then rose and entered the walk.

As I did so, I felt a great build-up of power and a vast increase in awareness. Colours and forms became more significant. I was aware of every single leaf on the bushes and trees, every blade of grass on the path standing out with startling clarity. It was as if physical reality had become much more real than it normally is, and the three-dimensional effect we are used to had become even more solid.

This kind of experience is impossible to describe in words. I had the impression of complete reality, and all that lies within and beyond it felt immediately immanent. There was an acute feeling of being one with nature in a complete way, as well as being one with the divine, which produced great exultation, and a deep sense of awe and wonder.

I became aware of Pan walking by my side and of a strong bond between us. He stepped behind me and then walked into me so that we became one, and I saw the surroundings through his eyes. At the same time, part of me—the recording, observing part—stood aside. The experience was not a form of possession but of identification, a kind of integration.

The moment he stepped into me the woods became alive with myriad beings—elementals, nymphs, dryads, fauns, elves, gnomes, fairies and so on, far too numerous to catalogue. They varied in size from tiny beings a fraction of an inch in height—like the ones I saw swarming about on a clump of toadstools—to beautiful elfin creatures, three or four feet tall. Some of them danced around me in a ring; all were welcoming and full of rejoicing. The nature spirits love and delight in the work they do and express this in movement.

I felt as if I were outside time and space. Everything was happening in the now. It is impossible to give more than a faint impression of the actuality of this experience, but I would stress the exultation and feeling of joy and delight. Yet, there was an underlying peace, contentment and a sense of spiritual presence.

I found myself in a clearing at the end of this part of the Rhododendron Walk, where there is a great oak tree. I turned and walked back the way I had come. I now had panpipes in my hands and was aware of shaggy legs and cloven hooves. I began to dance down the path, playing on the pipes—the melody I had heard Pan play before.

The numerous birds responded, their songs making an exquisite counterpoint to the music of the pipes. All the nature beings were active, many dancing as they worked. When I had almost reached the spot where the experience had started, the heightened awareness began to fade and Pan withdrew, leaving me once more my ordinary self. I stopped dancing and walked on. This was just as well, as there was a boy sitting on the seat under the cedar tree. He might have found it disconcerting if I had come dancing out of the path playing (what would have no doubt been to him) invisible pipes!

PAN'S WORLD

·

ROC

*Another meeting with Pan, in the public gardens at
St Annes-on-Sea in Lancashire a few days later, provided
further confirmation of the nature kingdom's openness and
willingness to communicate and cooperate with humankind.
Through Roc, Pan is expanding his message to touch other
people with his wisdom and power.*

I had gone there with several friends, including Peter Caddy, who were attending a conference. I was walking alone by a pond at one end of the gardens, across from the house, when I became aware of Pan standing beside me. As before, he stepped into me and I became one with him. Again, a recording and observing part of me stood aside.

This 'compound being'—Pan and myself—summoned the nature spirits together to help in what was to take place. The pond and all the bushes and trees became immediately alive with beings of many different kinds. I—or perhaps I should say 'we'—walked onto a raised part of the gardens from where it was possible to look across to the house where the meeting was taking place. There were again panpipes in my hands and I, or rather Pan within me, called upon the green ray of the nature forces to rise up through the house like sap rising up a tree trunk. Slowly this light rose until it emerged from the roof. After some time, Pan withdrew.

I left the garden and about five minutes later met Peter, who had just come from the house. He startled me by saying that Pan had been in the room and communicated with a certain woman present there who was a sensitive and that, of the fifteen others present in the room, nearly all had had visions or impressions connected with nature.

The significance of these two episodes became clearer in time. A reconciliation between humanity and the nature spirits is required for the survival of the world. For this reason Pan had to initiate a direct contact. As I see it, the main reason for my communication with the elementals was the contribution it made to the work of the Findhorn garden. By bringing onto a conscious level the links already existing there with nature spirits, I could receive guidance and knowledge complementary to Dorothy's link with the devic world. Thus, the aim of the Findhorn garden of full cooperation among the three kingdoms—the devas, the nature spirits and humanity—could be established and built up.

It is vital for the future of mankind that belief in the nature spirits and their god Pan is re-established and that they are seen in their true light. In spite of the outrages humanity has committed against nature, these beings are only too pleased to help us if we will seek and ask for their cooperation.

The nature spirits must be believed in with complete sincerity and faith. They must be appreciated and given thanks and love for the work they do. Let us try in our own ways to make friends with these wonderful beings and ask their help in making earth a beautiful and perfect place.

THE TRAVELLING ELF

·

BRIAN NOBBS

Roc's extraordinary presence had a profound effect on those around him, as Findhorn potter Brian Nobbs recalls. Roc enabled people to understand things they might have been entirely sceptical about, or which they longed to experience but felt unable to approach. In esoteric terms, Roc was a teacher who could cause perceptual changes in his student; these changes would then become permanent. Roc's presence also acted as a catalyst to help awaken Brian's ability to sense energies.

A few years after the amazing experiences of Roc and others at St Annes-on-Sea I was in Edinburgh to do some business with a ceramics supply company. Roc invited me to stay at his flat for the weekend. It would prove to be one of the most memorable weekends of my life.

Roc told me that he was sure there was a special reason for my being there at that time and that he had a prompting to take me to two places in Edinburgh that have strong nature associations: the Botanic Garden and the Hermitage of Braid by Blackford Hill.

On passing through the gate of the Botanic Garden he told me simply to report any impressions I received. He did not define this in any way. Immediately I found myself with a vivid feeling, as physical and undeniable as any sense impression ever is, of wading through a medium as resistant as flowing water but carrying a tingling electrical charge that flowed around my ankles and through my whole body. I felt as though I should be glowing! I was able to accurately identify the direction of flow of successive rivers of ley energy,[1] while Roc pointed out the various markers in the Edinburgh skyline visible from the Garden, with which they aligned. Among them was the Salisbury Crag (Arthur's Seat) and St Margaret's Chapel on the Castle Mount.

Then as we walked by the Modern Art Gallery in the Garden I became aware of an overwhelming presence I had never sensed before and realised that in my mind I could vividly see a stunning image of Pan, standing on the grassy mound in front of the gallery. Even though my eyes saw nothing, I could have rendered a picture of him in detail and colour.

I was diffident of telling Roc about this but I had stopped involuntarily and he turned to face me with an amused smile on his face. So I said, 'Is it . . . could it be Pan?'

'Yes,' he answered, 'and he wonders why it took you so long to pluck up the courage to speak. He welcomes you into his world!'

Since that moment, when he initiated contact from his side of the veil, I have been able to 'see' Pan and the other elementals that are his subjects.

From the Botanic Garden we went on to the Hermitage of Braid. As we approached the Hermitage I became aware of what seemed like an electrified breeze. It was strongly directional and as I indicated the direction for Roc he confirmed that it was energy radiating from the area of the Hermitage. This sign of strong activity filled us both with anticipation.

The small ravine that forms the Hermitage Walk is less than a mile in length and through it flows a small stream that twists and turns more than the ravine itself. There are many beautiful mature trees, some of them exotic but mostly native hardwoods. It is an extraordinarily beautiful place to find so close to the bustle of Edinburgh and is much used by dog strollers and joggers. On this day though there were hardly any people around. As we entered the walk a most extraordinary sensation began in the crown of my head. It was as though the top of my head opened and a beam of light descended into it producing a truly ecstatic feeling of wellbeing and bliss. There was something like the very clear high tone produced by a flute but carrying in its harmonics every imaginable musical sound. My feet suddenly seemed awkward to manage as though I were a little drunk, and as we walked I became aware that accompanying us were many small beautiful figures. There was no doubt in my mind that they were elves, but of some high order or rank. They seemed androgynous and very beautiful, wearing clothes like those depicted in fairy stories, in colours of russet, gold and green. They wore hats with high peaks and pointy shoes with curly toes. They were about three feet tall.

Again I felt a diffidence born of the strangeness to me of such experiences and waited quite a few minutes before telling Roc what I felt and saw. Meanwhile I had images of the elves pointing and giggling at my obvious discomfiture.

Roc said nothing but by now wore a knowing smile and was looking at me expectantly. So I told him and he confirmed that these were 'high elves', associated with trees and woodlands but having other, more esoteric functions in nature as guardian spirits and protectors of sacred places.

We all walked along in a kind of companionable silence, though the elves did not so much walk as dance. In my subsequent experience of these beings it has always been clear that they can scarcely contain the energy and joy that is their nature, and it is by no means unusual for them to be very playful and even childlike.

A little aside regarding the term 'high elf'. The term appears in the fantasies of Professor J.R.R. Tolkien, so it raises the question of which came first, the fantasy or the elf? My theory is that these beings use our categories to present themselves to us, since their essential being is probably incomprehensible and outside our experience, except that in our creation of imaginary worlds we may very well reflect hidden realities and make them more comprehensible to us. I am convinced that nature spirits are not in fact like little human beings, but have no fixed form and would most accurately manifest as constantly moving, shimmering rainbows of light.

So, we continued along in this way and finally came to the end of the walk. As we stood by the museum and information centre, the elves took their leave except for one of their number who stayed with us. Roc explained that he was to return with me to Findhorn where he would be making connections with energy from centres around Britain and the world, and would be helpful to the gardeners. As we waited for the bus to take us back to Roc's flat the elf disappeared.

The next morning I was waiting for the long-distance bus for Inverness. As it pulled into the kerb I suddenly realised that the elf was standing with me! He got on the bus and sat in the seat beside me. The feeling of incipient madness, consternation and sheer amusement that this gave me can be imagined. I was concerned that

AFTERNOON WITH A FAUN

someone might want to sit on the seat he was in and I really could not figure out whether I would have the courage to say, 'Excuse me but that seat is occupied.' In the end no one chose to sit there. Perhaps he had some way to influence them unconsciously?

I was met at Inverness by friends who brought me and the elf back to Findhorn. He seemed to enjoy the car. Obviously all this was for him unnecessary: he can be anywhere he wishes just by thinking about it. I believe that there is a humorous wish to show fellow-ship with our limitations, as well as a real interest in experiencing them. Perhaps a good analogy would be the way in which we might, on a beautiful day, enjoy walking to a destination instead of going by car.

The elf accompanied me to my caravan which I was sharing with a friend, Christian Torjussen. I had had no contact with Christian while I was in Edinburgh, so he knew nothing of my recent experiences. He was sitting reading as we arrived. As I opened the door the elf leapt into the caravan, did a sort of cartwheel and landed on the seat beside Christian, who reacted with astonishment to an invisible but felt presence.

His book dropped from his hands and he looked at the space beside him and said, 'What is it? Is it an elf?'

This event sharpened his sensitivity, though it was already well developed, and during the ensuing summer we both had incredible joy in a new and vivid awareness of this elf and many others of his kind. They took to riding on our shoulders; quite often we would sight each other with our elfin friends, and we would point and laugh—'You too!'

The garden team were delighted to hear this story and wanted to know the elf's name. It turned out that human language cannot cope with elvish names so they were invited to find him one. They came up with Merlando, which definitely sounded magical enough and which he accepted.

The sheer magic of that summer would be hard to describe. Forever transfigured by its high points, in memory it is filled with sunshine and the fragrance of flowers and much laughter; truly a taste of the next realm!

THE KING OF THE ELVES

Not all contact Roc had with the nature spirits proved joyful.
The Magic of Findhorn *relates a much darker experience*
Roc had with a group of elves.

On one occasion in 1967 Roc took Peter Caddy to the Black Isle, a beautiful peninsula north of Inverness, to see the Faerie Glen he had visited as a small boy. Roc remembered the place as lovely, enchanting, well-kept, but sixty years later the place was almost unrecognisable. It was completely neglected; fallen fences and overgrown trees barred their way. As Roc stared in disbelief at the forlorn glen, even the air seemed oppressive. Yet in spite of his shock and disappointment, he couldn't tear himself away. He felt there was something else there, just out of sight. Sensing this also, Peter went to move forward, but Roc motioned for him to stay where he was.

As Roc made his way forward, he felt increasingly ill at ease. His life energy began to drain away, until the sensation was almost unbearable. Pushing his discomfort aside he continued to look around him. He thought he saw something, but there was nothing in sight. The feeling he was not alone continued. He decided to remain where he was, and wait.

As he breathed in the rich smell of the earth and fallen pine needles, he felt strangely alive. Then, all at once it seemed as if his body was transforming— putting down roots, leaves sprouting from his hands.

These sensations continued until he felt an integral part of the green world around him. Then, out of this living green, two green figures appeared, challenging his presence there.

Taken aback at their hostility, Roc talked of his friendship with Pan, and his love of nature spirits. But the elves had no such love for mankind. Bows and arrows drawn, they ordered Roc to go back the way he had come. Though he knew he was in danger, Roc stood his ground, talking once more of his love and desire to help.

Then, to his relief, he became aware of Pan's presence. The elves lowered their bows and invited Roc forward. As he stared once more at the neglected place around him, Roc realised their hostility was born of a deep grief at what man had done here. After moving forward with them for a time, he decided to turn back.

That evening, under the light of a near full moon, Roc returned to the Faerie Glen. Making his way through the overgrown trees and rampant undergrowth, he came to where he had previously met the elves. Here, once more, his body became rooted to the earth, and his arms like branches. In amongst this living green he felt the sentience in the trees around him.

The two elves he had encountered earlier in the day reappeared, and took him into a glade, which filled with light as he approached. There waiting for him was a huge gathering of nature spirits. In the centre sat a single elf—clearly their king—who beckoned him forward through a sea of shimmering light. The air was alive with anticipation.

As Roc moved closer he became aware once more of the hostility he had experienced earlier. The anger of those present was mirrored in the elf king's eyes. As this powerful figure spoke, he talked of the terrible destruction caused by men, upsetting the balance of nature, harming animals, laying waste the land, vandalising the living earth. He saw mankind as a parasite, and challenged those who dared to ask for the cooperation of the nature spirits. Then the elf king demanded Roc justify himself.

It was a strange moment for Roc. As he paused to collect his thoughts, he was all too aware that until a year ago he had had no experience of nature spirits. And now here he was in front of this large gathering. How could he explain humankind?

He began by admitting the dark things men had done, but reminded the nature spirits this was not the full picture—that many humans were equally distressed about the terrible things being done to the earth. Then he asked that humans be treated fairly, and that the nature spirits help to bring humans a greater understanding and love of nature.

Roc then asked the elf king if the nature spirits could destroy humans. 'Easily,' was the elf king's response. He explained that if the nature spirits withdrew the vital force from nature, men could no longer survive. The elf king added that humans were just as capable of destroying themselves. Roc then spoke on behalf of men, assuring the elf king that humans were trying, they were 'turning within'.

At this the elf king's face lit up. He assured Roc elves would not hurt mankind, but that they were entitled to play tricks on humans when they come to places where they were not welcome, or if they sought to destroy; with that he faded into the hillside. As the lights faded, so too did all who had come there. And once more Roc was alone in the moonlight.

LIFE FORCE

·

ROC

*The closer Roc came to living nature, the more he understood
the responsibility we have to respect and care for the earth
and its nature spirits. In an excerpt from a talk he gave to the
Findhorn gardeners in March 1974, he speaks of the links
between the nature spirits and the life force itself.*

Findhorn is a very important place, a vitally important place. The Findhorn garden is very important
because one of the things that is essential in this moving
into the New Age is that man once more gets back the
sensitivity and contact which he once had with the
nature kingdom and its nature beings.

This contact was lost, and I think that it *had* to
be lost. Man had to develop his intellect. The more
he developed his intellect, however, the more he lost
his sensitivity, and of course reached a point where he
began to regard such things as a belief in nature spirits
or Pan or anything else as sheer superstition.

Now the time has come and man must get back
his sensitivity. There's a lot of evidence coming from
all over the world that in fact this is happening. Ever
so many people in many groups, the people who are
working for the Light, the people who are working for
spiritual purposes, are beginning to develop more and
more sensitivity. This doesn't mean that man is going
to lose his intellect. What's going to happen now is
that man is going to redevelop that sensitivity he lost,
the sensitivity he had to lose, but he is going to be able
to use it along with his intellect. This, of course, will
make him a very powerful being.

We know that man's situation on the earth is in rather a precarious position, because man has such a feeling of his own superiority to everything else. He has the belief, which of course you can find in the Bible, that he has dominion over all the other species. To be given dominion over anything doesn't mean that you can dominate that thing and force it to do what you think it ought to do. It means that you've got to develop an understanding of the thing you're dominating. You've got to understand it completely; you've got to have sympathy with it, you've got to love with it, so that above all you do not exploit it. Unfortunately, man has reached the state where he is not trying to cooperate with nature. He has the viewpoint: 'I have domination over nature. I am going to subdue nature. I am going to force nature to do what I want it to do.'

Of course, this particular attitude leads ultimately to total disaster, because a point will come when nature will revolt, and all sorts of things could happen. The nature spirits are tolerant to a degree which is very difficult to understand. They'll accept the most appalling outrages because they have infinite understanding, and they realise when man does something through ignorance and not through intention. Under such circumstances they'll show tolerance; they will not revolt, because they know that it is not according to God's will that they do so.

At the same time, there may come a point, if man goes too far, when they would decide: 'All right. We are tired and fed up with mankind. We'll go.' Now, a lot of people might say, 'What does it matter if a lot of hypothetical elves and gnomes leave the earth? It won't matter a bit. We know how to grow things; we'll go on growing. Everything will be fine.' So they would go on growing plants. They might go on growing them very well. But they would lack something, and that is life force. There would be no vitality. Therefore grains or fruits or vegetables grown without the help of the nature spirits would lack vitality. And therefore as foodstuffs they would not have much value.

This is the importance of trying to come into communication with—in trying to acquire a belief in—the nature kingdom. Because in fact not only can the nature spirits help with plant growth, but they can supply this vital energy. One of their functions, besides the building up of the etheric counterpart of the trees and plants, is to transmute the energy which has been directed down from the devas into the type of energy that is right for the particular plants, so that it goes into the right plant. This is the vital energy, which is the life energy.

A KALEIDOSCOPE OF GARDENS
·

ROC

As Roc's perceptions opened up he began to experience
nature in new ways. In June 1969 he experienced a powerful
vision involving several nature power places in Britain
while listening to Stravinsky's 'The Rite of Spring' in the
Findhorn sanctuary.

I have very odd experiences at times when I seem to be in two places at once. It is as if I leave my body and most of my consciousness goes too. Last night listening to the playing of 'The Rite of Spring', one of the most profound examples of pure nature music, I found myself with Pan in the garden at Quarry Wood near Newbury, Berkshire. There were myriads of elementals and nature spirits all over the garden. All seemed to be dancing joyously; there was a tremendous feeling of exultation. We visited three parts of the garden, the first being a large expanse of grass with a long straight path down the middle, and on this path a stone urn had been placed over a nature power point. At right angles to this is another straight path, part of which is known as the Nun's Walk, which runs beside a stream to a wild corner where the stream turns at right angles. This is apparently Pan's special place. The third place was a higher part of the garden, grassy with trees, a very strong centre of fairies and elves.

Next I was aware of being with Pan at Attingham Park on the Mile Walk in front of the huge oak tree The Ancient of Days, on which there is a bronze plaque with the Hymn to Pan in green on it. Again I was aware of the presence of the nature spirits and elementals, all with great joy and happiness.

Then I was on the Fairy Mound in Jessica Ferriera's garden on Iona and at St Catherine's Chapel in Windermere in the Lake District. Pan was still with me, and the dancing nature spirits. The next place was the wild section of the Botanic Garden in Edinburgh, which is a focal point of the nature spirits. After that I was walking through the wood on Dorothy Howard's estate at Rhu on the river Clyde, west of Glasgow, where there was a tremendous feeling of power and rejoicing.

Then I was in the well-known gardens at Inverewe on the west coast of Scotland in a high part of the garden, which again is a focal centre. From there I was in a centre point in the extraordinary forest near Ullapool, which is a tree devic centre for Scotland. After that I was aware of being in two powerful nature centres in Scotland: the Corrieshallock Gorge, and the Falls of Rogie, an extremely powerful water spirit centre.

Then I was in the wild part of Kincorth, a garden not far from Findhorn, which incidentally was the place where I was first told of the importance of every garden having a wild section which acts as a focal point for the nature spirits to work from and which they feel is theirs. Then Blackhills near Elgin, on a high part of the garden, which again is a very strong power point. From there to a garden at Williamston, at the place where the path that contains the power points crosses to the avenue of trees. Then finally I was in the wild part of the garden here at Findhorn.

Then an extraordinary thing happened. It was as if all the different places I had visited were one. They seemed to be united and yet separate, as if interweaving in a kaleidoscopic way.

I finally ended up on a very heavily wooded conical hill, the top of which was free from trees and in the centre of which was a stone, an altar to nature. I could get no inner guidance as to where this place is. I am not certain if it exists on this earth or is a place on another plane, but if I ever come across it I shall know it at once.

It would seem from this experience that the gardens where the nature forces are working, and where in some cases there are nature power points, are being linked up so that there can be an interchange of the forces and powers at work.

MAGIC ON MIDSUMMER EVE
·

ROC

*Over the years Roc had many encounters with Pan and his
subjects. Through his conversations with Pan he gained
greater understanding of his experiences with the nature
spirits and of the 'web of life'.*

In June 1972 I went to the Royal Botanic Garden in Edinburgh in the early afternoon. It was Midsummer Eve, an important day for the nature spirits. A dull day, but there were blinks of sunshine. I came into the Garden from Inverleith Row by the east gate and took the path to the left, leading to the rock garden. I stopped to look at a horse chestnut which has always fascinated me because of the strange markings on the bark which look like hieroglyphics or ancient native carvings. I am sure they mean something but so far I have not been able to decipher them.

A little beyond this tree, I left the path and went up the grassy slope to go on through the heath garden, which was suddenly alive with nature spirits. Green elves, three to four feet tall, were walking in front of me, full of joy and delight, and little gnomes were running about almost under my feet. Kurmos came towards me from amongst the bushes; still the beautiful little faun who was my first contact with these beings. He greeted me with joy and, turning, danced off in front of me between the elves.

Pan was with me, very powerful, on my left as I walked on to the top of the heath garden towards the 'Tree of Life'. This tree—*Zelkova carpinifolia*, referred to as the Tree of Life[1] by Richard St Barbe Baker, the Man of the Trees—is a strange tree which I like to greet when I go to the Garden. Even this specimen, which is not large, has a powerful energy field.

I walked round it clockwise and then stood looking at a section of the bark just below the level of my head. My attention was caught by a group of markings on the bark that were in the form of a figure about fourteen inches high. I had often looked at this tree, but had never seen this effect. The figure was distinct. It was strange and slightly sinister—a faun-like being with longish straight horns; the eyes were quite noticeable. I had been aware of the tree spirit but had never seen it before. Was this a representation of it on the bark?

A mist formed between me and the tree and I found myself looking at the entity itself, standing in front of the tree. He was about my own height, thickset and dark-skinned. His eyes, which were fierce, challenged me. 'Afraid?'

'No.'

'Would you have felt so drawn to my tree if you had seen me before?'

'Yes, I think so.'

'Will you touch the tree as you have always done, aware this time that you are doing it through me?'

I laid my hand on the trunk of the tree and felt the usual strong flow of energy.

'Will you lean your back against the tree, again through me?'

I did so and was aware of a strange warming energy.

'You find me odd—not what you expected. You are not repulsed?'

'I am disconcerted. You certainly are not what I expected, but I love this tree and you are the tree, you are not evil.'

'I am neither good nor evil. My tree has been called the Tree of Life. I am what you make of me.'

I moved away from the tree and turned round. I was aware of the tree spirit standing against the trunk where I had been leaning—strong, powerful and strange. In spite of his appearance I felt an activation of the heart centre.

Pan, who had moved away from me as I approached the tree, was again beside me. 'You are developing in the right direction,' he said, smiling. 'More and more easily you are able to accept the stranger-looking of my subjects with discernment, being aware of the true quality of the elemental and not put off by the apparently sinister aspect. Able, instead, to feel love and respect.'

'I have always felt a special attraction for this tree, ever since I first came across it some years ago. When I lean against the trunk I draw much energy from it.'

'Seeing this aspect of the tree spirit has made no difference?'

'No. The energy field of the tree is unchanged.' I looked at Pan enquiringly. 'You said "this aspect of the tree spirit", meaning he has others?'

'Yes, he has others. The form in which he shows himself is suited to the occasion. It has a purpose.'

'To test my reaction? Or to disconcert me?'

Pan smiled. 'Perhaps a bit of both. Your reaction was good. Where do you want to go next?'

I indicated a path that skirts the south side of the rock garden, and we proceeded along it. Kurmos and the elves were still ahead of us in the distance. Most of the clouds had dispersed and the sun was shining; I felt great happiness.

Some distance ahead, where the path is bordered by bushes and trees, there was an empty seat, but before sitting down I decided to visit the redwood trees which I love so much. There are six or seven of them arranged in a rough circle. These trees radiate a quite different kind of energy than any other tree. They are young trees, not yet very large, but they are beautiful.

Kurmos and the elves had disappeared and Pan was no longer with me. A seat near the trees was occupied by a man reading a paper, and a long-haired youth was sitting on the ground near a border, sketching flowers. I could not very well embrace the trees as I would like to have done, or even talk to them, except mentally. I walked round them and then stood for a few moments in the centre of the circle, before returning to the seat I had seen. It was, of course, now occupied; it was obviously not the right place for me. As I turned towards another path which curved round a rhododendron bush, Kurmos came running out of it and beckoned to me.

He turned and I followed him along the curving path to an empty seat. The path was narrow and I felt enclosed by trees and bushes and very close to nature. I watched two bullfinches in the bush opposite. Some sparrows came twittering down onto the path, hoping perhaps for breadcrumbs. A blackbird was hopping about almost in front of me and a squirrel dashed across the path and climbed about a yard up a tree trunk, disappearing round the back of it. It must have jumped into a bush close by as I could see its tail, which then remained motionless for some time. The tail then disappeared with a flick, after which the squirrel came out from under another bush onto the edge of the path. It sat up, looking at me, came a few feet towards me and then, turning, scampered off. Kurmos, who had been standing in the middle of the path watching, came and sat beside me.

'This reminds me of our first meeting when you asked me why human beings are so stupid.'

Kurmos looked up at me with a mischievous grin. 'You can't answer that question, can you?'

'No, I can't. Since I have come to see the human race through the eyes of beings like yourself, I sometimes wonder how you can put up with us at all.'

'We find human behaviour amusing at times, but so often it is destructive, cruel and horrible, or so it appears to us; it makes us sad. We try to understand but it isn't easy. We know there are those who love nature, who love this garden and find happiness and peace amongst the flowers, bushes and trees; who love the birds and the squirrels and feed them with crumbs and nuts. No doubt they would love us if they could see us. This makes us happy and we draw near to them. Some of them may even be aware of us, though they cannot see us. Why can you see us so clearly?'

'I suppose because I am a privileged person, one of those chosen to link with Pan and help to renew the old contact between mankind and the nature spirits.'

Pan appeared at that moment, standing opposite us. 'You were chosen because you are suited to the task. Your entire life has been a training and preparation for this and for other things. As soon as the integration between your lower self and your higher self reached a certain degree of completion you were bound to see us. Your lower self and your physical body had to be trained and conditioned for many years before this level could be reached. To see and communicate with us in the way you do requires just as much training as the skilled brain surgeon or virtuoso musician. You know well how long it has taken—and we are speaking only of this life.'

Kurmos looked up at me. 'Now I understand,' he said. He rose and turned to Pan who placed his hand on the little faun's head and looked down at him with infinite affection in his eyes.

'You, too, were chosen for the part you played in bringing about our meeting, my little henchman.'

A slow, beatific smile spread over the faun's face. He appeared to grow in stature. He gave a cry, spun round and went dancing along the path. Pan looked after him, smiling, then crossed the path and sat beside me. 'Your work must have its problems.'

'Yes, many problems, mainly interesting ones, often amusing, sometimes disconcerting. Now that I accept the fact that what is happening is real, I am becoming used to the problems. There was a time when I doubted, when it seemed to me that the whole thing might be a fantasy, projections from my own unconscious. But to think of you as a projection from a part of my own unconscious—or as a secondary personality, as the clever all-knowing psychologist might maintain—seems to me totally ridiculous.'

'Are you sure?'

'Yes, I am sure. A great being like yourself could never be part of my unconscious.'

Pan looked at me with a curious smile, a smile I knew well. 'Have you never felt that I was within you?'

'Oh yes, there were the times when you walked into me as you did on the Mile Walk at Attingham and I saw the outside world through your eyes.'

'Would you say I "possessed" you?'

'No, it was not "possession", which usually implies something unpleasant or evil. It was identification, a kind of integration which is quite different from possession.'

'Apart from those times, have you never felt that I was somehow within you?'

'Yes, yes, of course I have.' I looked at him. 'Now I understand what you mean. We are told to "turn within", to seek God within, to seek Christ within. But this within-ness is not contained in my physical body, which would limit it; it is in all dimensions of space and time, it is infinite, it is the eternal now. We turn away from the outside world, the material world which so many believe to be the only reality, to seek that other reality, the true reality which is within and yet is everywhere.'

Pan, by his questions, had released a deep inner knowledge from my unconscious mind where it had been stored. It was now flowing out in a way that surprised myself. 'In that sense, of course,' I continued, 'you are within me, the whole universe is within me, the elemental kingdom, the angelic hierarchy. Christ is within me, God himself is within me. This within-ness is the All, the great mystery which we poor humans cannot hope to understand completely. We can only grope towards it and in some way seek to apprehend it. If we believe it is possible to do this we will find what we seek: at least a facet of the ultimate truth.'

Pan placed his hand on my arm. 'Looked at in one way, your "clever, all-knowing psychologist" is right. I am within you, but the projection is unnecessary. To turn within in the right way and to centre oneself on the cosmic Christ is to develop cosmic consciousness and bring about integration between the lower and higher selves. When a certain degree of this development has been reached and you turn without, to the contemplation of the material world through the medium of the physical senses, you see it in a different way because you are now aware of, and in touch with, the true reality behind it.

'Because of the Ray you are on, and the work you have to do, you see me and my subjects as if we were part of the material world. This is not projection; it is bringing cosmic reality into manifestation when it is right to do so, for, of course, you do not see us as part of the material world all the time; that would be too much. Your physical body could not take it and it would lead to confusion. It happens for a reason when it is necessary and will increase your understanding of the elemental kingdom, in which case your sensitivity is stepped up to bring it about and one or more of us will become visible to you as required. Only on rare occasions, such as on the Mile Walk at Attingham where you say I stepped into you, do you see the lot—or at least as much of it as you can take.' Pan looked at me with a twinkle.

'Can you explain the mechanism?' I asked. 'I am certain it is not due to heightened sensitivity of physical sight only.'

'It is a mixture of that plus an added higher vision brought about by the development of cosmic consciousness.'

'That makes sense to me. But I am unable to control it myself. For instance, I cannot wish to see a nature spirit and immediately do so, however hard I try.'

'It is done from our side when it is right for you to have this heightened vision or when a particular entity wishes to become visible to you.'

'How is that done?'

Pan laughed and shrugged his shoulders. 'There you go again with your questions.'

'How else can I find out? I want to know, that is, if it is possible to explain to a three-dimensional mortal who can only use a small part of his brain.'

'All right, I'll do my best by an analogy. Imagine a theatre with a large stage.'

'A theatre! My dear Pan, what do you, the god of the elemental world, know about man's places of entertainment?'

'All that is necessary. Remember, I am everywhere. Have you forgotten the time when I sat in the empty seat beside you at a performance of *A Midsummer Night's Dream* at the Edinburgh Festival?'

I laughed delightedly. 'I have not. You liked the little Welshman's Puck?'

'It was acceptable. But to return to my analogy, which you interrupted: the stage is in darkness. It is thronged with people, but you cannot see them because of the darkness, which symbolises your lack of sensitivity. A narrow-beam spotlight picks out one of them and he immediately becomes visible to you. Any number of different individuals can be picked out and become visible in this way. Similarly, lights could pick out a group or the whole stage could be lit. The light symbolises your heightened senses. It is a rough analogy but it may answer your question.'

'It does. The lights are controlled by some being on your side, I take it?'

'Yes.'

'Therefore I can't select the entities I am to see or when. But I am aware of and can communicate with your subjects.'

'Of course, you can do this at any time, though you may only be able to see us on special occasions. The moment you think of an entity you are in immediate communication with it. You may or may not be aware of the response, according to your degree of sensitivity at the time, but it will almost certainly be there.'

'Can anyone make such a contact?'

'Yes, anyone can and it is important that this should be understood. The one-way contact is always there, but being aware of the response usually needs training or at least practice. It is very subtle and easily missed.'

'What saddens me is when others—fortunately not many—are envious of the gift I have been given. Why was I chosen? Why not them? It isn't fair. But there are many people who would genuinely and sincerely like to share my experiences and I am frequently asked how they can set about it.'

'And you hedge and say, "Someday you probably will if your faith is strong enough. Don't try too hard. It will just happen at the unexpected moment."'

I laughed. 'No doubt you have heard me at it?'

'I certainly have, and it is sound advice. You also tell them to follow your example and live in comparative isolation in the country for ten years as you did yourself.'

'I do, and most of them look aghast and say they could not possibly do that, they haven't the time and it might mean giving up too much.'

'There are people who want the easy way every time. "How to See Fairies in Six Simple Lessons." There is always time for the important things. Communicating with my subjects is not a garden game for the odd half hour when there is nothing better to do. It is of vital importance for the survival of mankind. Unless humanity comes to realise the dangerous stupidity of outraging nature and stops the ever-increasing rate of pollution it will ultimately destroy itself. Seeking cooperation between the three kingdoms—the devic,

nature and humanity—as is an aim at Findhorn, is
one way of helping mankind to survive. In your case,
if you had not spent those years at Cowford Cottage
you would never have seen either me or any of my
subjects. It was a basic necessity.

'Another question that arises in the desire to communicate with elemental beings is the motive behind it.
Curiosity is an important quality when it is the right
sort of curiosity, such as seeking after truth. There is
another kind—idle curiosity, wanting to know what
is going on, not to find out truth or useful information
but just to probe. How nice it would be to be able to
see lots and lots of harmless little fairies and dear little
gnomes dancing about in the garden. Of course they
have very little power, but they are such fun—dear
little pets that don't need any looking after.'

Pan seemed to swell in size and the power radiating from him stepped up. 'I have observed far too
much of this contemptuous, superior attitude of
humanity towards my subjects; it is almost worse
than disbelief. The smallest of them has more potential
power than the strongest human being. It is lucky for
mankind that we are infinitely tolerant and understanding and that we obey God's will. If we used a

fraction of the power we have we could wipe the whole of mankind off the face of the earth.

'We are not here to be the slaves of humanity but to collaborate with it to bring about a world of peace, cooperation and brotherly love, a world free from wars and violence. Humanity's disbelief in our existence does not destroy us—it can never do that. We are here and we shall always be here, even if humanity destroys itself and its material planet.

'Humanity is losing its dominion over the other kingdoms with which it shares the earth by its destructive behaviour, selfishness and stupidity. It is time humanity looked and saw what it is doing. It must face up to the consequences of its behaviour, which it cannot escape. If it does not, a time will come when only actions will teach you the necessary lessons. By then it may be too late!'

I drew a deep breath. 'My dear Pan, your power is terrifying. You have almost blasted me out of existence.'

His stern face relaxed into a smile. 'I'm sorry, I certainly have no wish to do that. Even I sometimes get carried away by anger. Let's leave it at that and return to the genuine people who are legitimately curious about my world and would dearly love to see us. There is nothing wrong with that except that it very rarely works—they try too hard. Perhaps this is fortunate as they do not realise how dangerous it might be if their desire was granted too soon, before their bodies or their minds had been prepared and conditioned for the experience, and the right degree of cosmic consciousness had been reached. The elementals, the ones who are my subjects, belong to a different evolutionary stream than humanity. Close contact between human beings and the elementals can be dangerous if it takes place too soon, especially if the motives for seeking it are wrong.

'My subjects are strange beings, as you well know. But really close links are only necessary with those who have special work to do. Many people who believe in the nature spirits and love them can be aware of them, can communicate with them and sometimes even see them in brief glimpses. With such people they will always cooperate when invoked, which simply means asking for help. This simple awareness is open to anyone who seeks it. It is the complete, total link that must be initiated from our side when it is required.'

'What would happen to an unprepared person who tried to make the close link, or to someone with the wrong motives?' I asked.

'Such a link is easily enough made but it would be on the wrong level with the wrong type of being, probably on the lower astral plane.'

'Tell me more about this. So far we have been talking about the pure elementals whose basic "light" bodies are vortexes of energy which I believe to belong to the angelic hierarchy, and who take on etheric bodies formed of substance drawn from the etheric shell of the earth in order to carry out their functions. These are the bodies that become personified as elves, fauns, fire elementals, air and water spirits and so on, such as are preserved as thought forms in man's myths and legends. As well as these I know there are other entities of a different type which I have referred to as pseudo-elementals.'

'You certainly know that they exist as you can both see and communicate with them and have sometimes had to deal with them—goblins, the black sort; imps; and a whole collection of nightmare horrors we need not go into.'

'They are not your subjects then?'

Pan gave me a look of horror. 'Certainly not. I wouldn't acknowledge them.'

'Do they have a god, or a leader of some sort?'

Pan sighed. 'Yes, unfortunately, my opposite. Call him Anti-Pan if you like, though it sounds odd. Everything about him is odd. You might regard him as a debased aspect of myself, a detached shadow. We're quite good friends in a way as he has a necessary part to play. I keep him at arm's length.'

'Is he at all like you?'

'Well, yes, in a debased sort of way. His horns are longer and vicious looking. He has real goat's legs and coarse hair. He smells of goat. He is the real nymph-chasing satyr, the goat-god, the true model for the devil. He is very earthy. Unfortunately too many people take him for me; that is the reason for the bad reputation I have in some quarters.'

'Is it easy to contact him?'

'Too easy. Invoke him with the right noises and he'll be there, masquerading as me.'

'What can you do about it?'

'More than you think but I usually leave it, unless he goes too far. The fools who invoke him deserve what's coming to them.'

'But do they know what they are doing?'

'Not always. But the truth comes to the surface in the end. There is too much negative energy involved. It shows. The balance is invariably upset and brings about consequences that cannot be ignored.'

'What sort of people can invoke him?'

'All sorts. Very often beautiful people with the highest ideals and good intentions, but they are earth oriented and have some kind of negative quality about them. Their cosmic consciousness is not highly developed, if at all.'

'Is he evil?'

'Not necessarily. That depends on how he is invoked and by whom, but he is a negative entity who brings negative energies with him. As I said, he has a role to play. But that's enough. I don't like talking about him.'

And on that last word, Pan withdrew. That is to say he disappeared from my sight. I spent some time walking about the Botanic Garden, thinking over our conversation, and then I went home.

ENCHANTMENTS OF AUTUMN

·

ROC

Another meeting took place in the Botanic Garden in October of the same year. As on the previous occasion, I had gone to the Garden in the early afternoon. This time I went to the rock garden itself and walked through it, absorbing its special atmosphere. As I reached the end of it and crossed the path, I was more conscious than usual of the livingness of the trees and bushes ahead of me, and of a closeness to and identification with the earth and the whole vegetable kingdom. I went across the grass in the direction of my favourite redwood trees.

After greeting the trees as I usually do, I went on by a grass path through the trees and bushes, conscious of an ever-increasing intensity of feeling causing my whole body to tingle and giving the experience I have described before as 'more real than real'; that intense 'three-dimensional-ness' that produces a feeling of ecstasy.

I came out of the path onto more open ground and went diagonally down the slope. As I did so I experienced a tremendous feeling of exultation. Such experiences are difficult to express in words and can never be adequately recounted. Only a pale reflection of the actual experience gets across and one has a sense of frustration because there is a shortage of the right, meaningful words to give it true expression.

When I reached the path I was making for, I crossed it and went to a seat a little way beyond it on the grass, where I sat and looked at the nearby trees. How vitally alive they were, though some of them had lost nearly all their leaves. I immediately became aware that not only were they alive but they were communicating with me; the trees themselves, that is, not the tree spirits or the nature beings still working with them.

I was not only overwhelmed by the love they were sending out, but realised that they were giving me thanks for the work I was being used for in passing on knowledge to people about the consciousness and sensitivity of the vegetable kingdom and the reality of the elemental helpers. The trees claimed me as one of themselves. This feeling of total oneness with all nature was wonderful. The unexpected appreciation was deeply moving. I now felt that my life had been worthwhile.

Pan was sitting beside me looking at me with amused affection. There was a sense of timeless wonder. The garden was full of nature beings. I expressed surprise at seeing so many at this time of year.

'Look at the number of trees that still have leaves on them. There is plenty of work to be done. Don't you think this is a beautiful time of the year?'

'I certainly do. The autumn colourings are superb.'

'How do you think the changes in colour are brought about? Who are the artists responsible for them?'

I looked at him in surprise. 'Do you mean your subjects are responsible? I had never thought of that.'

'Yes, my subjects are responsible. They are, as you see, superb artists. Of course the botanist will tell you differently. He has his explanation—I have mine. Which do you think is right? Take your choice.'

'Both are probably right. It all depends on the way you look at it.'

Pan laughed. 'Both are right. You develop in wisdom.'

'I have good teachers.'

Pan stood up and laughed again. 'Come, let us move on.'

I rose from the seat and we began to walk in the direction of the west gate. There was one part of the garden I felt we had to go to which I always think of as Pan's special place; a wild part, though it is not so wild now as it used to be. The grass, which was once allowed to grow, has been cut short. In spite of this it has lost nothing of its mysterious atmosphere.

We passed the road leading to the gate and as we walked on Pan turned to me and said: 'All the time you lived at Cowford Cottage you were unaware of the existence of such beings as nature spirits, in spite of your lifelong interest in esoteric and occult subjects?'

'At that time I would have dismissed belief in the real existence of fairies, gnomes or elves as superstition, or figments of the imagination.'

'A result of your scientific training?'

'I tried hard to find rational explanations for all the psychic phenomena I had come across and studied. But there were certain phenomena I had to accept which I could not explain away. Why are you asking these questions? You must be able to read my mind, so you already know the answers.'

'I ask the questions because I want you to re-examine the way you thought then and the philosophy you were developing.'

'That belongs to my past life. Is it important now?'

'You must never underestimate or despise the past. No doubt some of it can be discarded, but in reviewing your memories of those vital years of your life you will see how the bridges were built between your exoteric and esoteric ideas and experiences, and the way they have been integrated. By studying how this was brought about in your case, you may be able to help others to build their bridges.'

'I see. I suppose I have always believed that the past is important.'

'As a scholar of many years' experience and deep study, you know it is. Those who throw away the riches of tradition do so at their peril. You can't flout tradition. If you discard it, you build on sand.'

We walked on in silence, then Pan asked: 'Did you believe in me in those days?'

'As a boy I loved both the Greek myths and their Norse equivalents. The gods of both mythologies were very real to me. Yet, if anyone had suggested that I might one day see, talk to and even touch one of them, I would have burst out laughing and said, "Utter rubbish." And yet . . . I wonder.'

'Perhaps the strong desire to find a scientific, rational explanation for the unusual phenomena you were interested in was a surface veneer, part of the materialistic phase you went through—the "I only believe what I see and can demonstrate" period you have spoken about. It never succeeded in eradicating a deep, fundamental belief in the true reality, which was always there.'

'As a kid I passionately believed in fairies until it was suppressed by school life and replaced by an irrepressible curiosity to find out how and why things worked, and what became almost an obsessional interest in physics and chemistry.'

'Your original belief was suppressed but not destroyed. What was I to you then? With your interest in mythology you must have known about me. Was I the nymph-chasing satyr, the being who produced a feeling of panic in woods, an evil spirit, a devil?'

'No, none of these. You were the Pan of that wonderful chapter, "The Piper at the Gates of Dawn", in Kenneth Grahame's *The Wind in the Willows*.'

I stopped speaking and stared at him as something elusive rose into my consciousness from the depths of the unconscious. 'Surely you have always been the wonderful and beautiful being you are to me now. Is that why?'

'It is the reason why you were not afraid of me when I appeared to you, one of the reasons why you were chosen.'

We came to a seat beside a tree, not very far from the special corner we were making for, and sat down.

'My appearance must have come as a surprise to you.'

I laughed. 'Of course it did, but luckily for me, seeing and talking to the little faun Kurmos broke the shock it might otherwise have been.' I looked at him. 'You are an awesome being; you radiate such a power, but you are not frightening—at least to me. I must always have felt love for you; otherwise, as a human being, I would certainly have been afraid.'

'But you were not, and in you I found what I was looking for—a mediator who could be used to help to bring about the reconciliation between humanity and my kingdom and also to try to lift the stigma that was imposed on me by the early church. The coming years will show to what extent that is happening.'

We sat in silence for some time.

'Will a time ever come when I might lose contact with you and the elemental beings? If, for example, I had other work to do?'

'You have other work to do, as you already know but you will never lose contact with me. That bond, once made, is for ever. Wherever you are, I shall be, for

I am everywhere. You could not break the bond even if you wanted to. One of my functions is to look after you, to protect you, to take care of your physical body and help you in your work, my dear beloved brother. I am one of those who overlight you. As for the elementals, my subjects, they accept you, they acknowledge you, and they love you. They will never let you go.'

I smiled wryly. 'And what of the ancient legends and ballads that tell of the fate of a mortal man who gets involved with "fairie lands" and the Little People? Disappearing into the hollow hills for years like Rip Van Winkle or Thomas the Rhymer?'

'And what of the Hobbits and the elves of Rivendell? Of Lothlorien, of Celeborn and Galadriel? Are they not the best of company? So far you have not vanished into any hollow hills, at least not for long.'

'You read Tolkien?'

'My literary tastes are impeccable.' He smiled enigmatically at me. 'I don't read of course, but in a way I am involved. I suppose you know that you are closer to the elves than any of the others of my subjects? Do you feel lost?'

'No, I do not feel "lost". I believe in God, my link with the cosmic Christ is strong, I am dedicated to work for the Light. All the same, I feel in some ways "different".'

'You can't be anything else, because of what has happened to you. Does it worry you?'

'No. It is part of the price I have to pay and I do it willingly.' I looked at him and grinned. 'I don't have any choice, do I?'

'Not much. We chose you, and yet . . . you began it yourself.'

'Explain. How and when?'

'You'll find out some day. You must have patience.' Pan gave another of his strange, enigmatic smiles.

I shrugged. 'I need plenty of that,' and then I laughed. Sitting there perfectly still, in a state of greatly expanded awareness and sensitivity, with the mounting joy this produced, overwhelmed by the love pouring over me from this beautiful being beside me, and from all the nature spirits in the Garden, many of whom had gathered round us, as well as from the trees, bushes and plants, I felt so deeply moved I could not speak. It was almost more than my physical body could take.

Pan, fully aware of what was happening to me, took both my hands in his and looked into my eyes. The feelings did not lessen, but a profound peace, tranquillity and wonder was added. I was totally unaware of the passing of time.

At last, speaking with difficulty, I said, 'You seem to feel this bond with my lower self, my conscious ego, just as much as with my higher self. I am overwhelmed by this tremendous flow of love.'

'Of course, it has to be so.' He had released my hands but was still looking into my eyes. 'My relationship with your higher self cannot be expressed. It can only be understood on higher levels.' He rose. 'Let us go to the far corner, the one you call my corner.'

I rose too and we walked over the grass.

'To me you are so real.' I looked round at one or two people walking about in the Garden. 'In fact, in some strange way you are more real than those people who can't even see you.'

He glanced at me. 'Of course I am more real.'

Somehow the thought of this eternal true reality being mainly rejected by man depressed me. It was as if I experienced a sudden reaction from the previous joy. 'Humanity has developed its intellect for what? We believe that humanity lost its sensitivity and was cut off from contact with the other kingdoms and with God in order to do so. What has the so-called development of intellect led to? Greater and greater ability to trick, cheat and destroy our fellow men and exploit the earth and the other kingdoms for our own selfish ends. How can you and your subjects bear to share the earth with us? There are times when I am bitterly ashamed of my fellow human beings.'

Pan put an arm round my shoulder. 'Come now, you mustn't look on the black side like this. Your higher self must be off duty. I shall have to take his place. It is true that humanity has done and is doing terrible things as you say. But he is also doing great and beautiful things. Many humans reach great spiritual heights in their lifetime; sometimes they are great beings in incarnation. Concentrate on the good and the beautiful. Turn your back on the sensational headlines. Read inspiring books, of which you have many, listen to great music and lose yourself in fine paintings. Never forget that great art, in every sense of the word—literature, music, painting and so on—contains behind it the true reality, the eternal truth, the spiritual teachings and, in some cases, the basic truths of the Ancient Wisdom, and is a source of the great esoteric teachings, though concealed in symbolic terms.'

'Of course you are right. But it is difficult to understand why so many people despise art, failing to realise its purpose, and, in spite of their boasted enlightened intellect and civilised behaviour, take the true reality for imagination and hallucination and believe that the illusory is the real.'

Pan smiled. 'Like Plato's men in the cave turning their backs on the truth and taking the shadows on the wall for reality.'

I laughed. The sudden black mood had passed. 'What, Pan talking of Plato?'

'Why not? After all, I am Greek, and proud of our philosophers. At least, my seeming appearance is Greek, though my origin is much older. Talking of my appearance, what do you feel when people say I must be ugly?'

'Disgusted and horrified, though I realise that few if any of them have actually seen you. What they are criticising is an imaginary picture conjured up from the description of you as half human and half animal, with horns and cloven hooves. I must not blame the human imagination for its lapses. I often wish they could see the reality as I do. You are a being of incredible beauty.'

The mischievous twinkle appeared in Pan's eyes. 'Gross flattery will get you nowhere.'

'It happens to be the truth.'

'Unfortunately my debased counterpart, Anti-Pan, has received most attention from artists, because he is more easily contacted and, as you suggest, human imagination where I am concerned tends to be gross. And so the wrong image of me is perpetuated and I am depicted with exaggerated horns, a beard and animal legs, usually goat's. It is unimportant. I prefer not to be represented in any material form. Unfortunately, the pictures of my opposite can channel negative energies and could even, at times, be evil, depending on the personality and degree of spiritual development of the artist.'

By this time we had reached the special corner I associated so strongly with Pan and we stood in silence for a time.

'I regret that they have cut the grass,' I said presently. 'I much preferred it long. This is too trim.'

Pan shrugged his shoulders. 'It doesn't matter very much. I agree with you but this garden has been here for a very long time and we have established a focal centre so strongly that there is little the most enthusiastic trimmers and pruners could do to alter it now.'

'What about the garden at Findhorn? Suppose they intruded on the wild part—would that make any difference now?'

'It certainly would. Findhorn is a special place where the three-part cooperation, between devas, nature spirits and humans, started. Even if the wild part had been established as it is now for a hundred years of your time it would be unwise to disturb it, and to do so would affect the rest of the garden adversely.'

'I thought so. How is the cooperation working from your point of view?'

'Rather shakily at times. Through Dorothy, with her devic contacts, and you from the nature spirits, much guidance and advice has been given. The main principles for the successful cooperation have been given. The attitude towards the work has been made clear, and things to avoid which do damage to the soil or the plants also made clear. Inevitably mistakes have been made from time to time, but as long as they are noticed and the lessons learnt they have had their uses. Whether the principles and laws that have been given are followed or not is man's part. It is up to the gardeners at Findhorn.

'Because of the importance of this garden we watch with attention and interest. The garden is an astonishing one but occasionally things are done from expediency or self-interest which we can't accept, as they are offensive and a breach of the laws that have been given. We are infinitely tolerant and understanding but because Findhorn is the starting point of the cooperation we can't overlook wrong actions as we can in gardens where there is ignorance about us. When the wrong things are done consequences follow.'

'What sort of consequences?'

'Many sorts. Changes in the soil, or infestation with greenfly, caterpillars and other garden pests or diseases that attack plants. The Findhorn garden is important as an actual demonstration of what can take place where a true cooperation between the kingdoms is achieved, and where humanity is aware of its responsibility towards other kingdoms and ceases to exploit them. Already the Findhorn garden has had a good deal of publicity but that is nothing compared with what may well happen in the next few years. It would be unfortunate if it lapsed from its special state.'

'Is that possible? It is noted for the vitality and radiance of its plants.'

'Unfortunately it is possible. If for any reason the wrong energies were channelled into it, the present vitality could be impaired. There is no need to dwell on something that is obvious. It is not likely to happen, but a careful watch must be kept. The gardeners at Findhorn must have very special qualities. They are of course human and cannot help the occasional lapse from the ideal. We make allowances for that.'

'What sort of qualities do they need?'

'To begin with, one that is fundamental to the whole of the Findhorn community. Total dedication to work for the Light under God's guidance. Turning within to seek that guidance and develop cosmic consciousness. Seeking to further universal love and the brotherhood of man and to search unremittingly for the truth.

'Special qualities are love of the earth and all vegetation; love of the work that has to be done; a determination to respect the earth and all growing things and to refrain from using chemicals and undue force to modify or alter the natural growth of plants, constantly remembering that plants are living things with a high degree of sensitivity; a total acceptance of the reality of the elemental kingdom and of the possibility of the success of the three-part cooperation which is one of the basic aims of the Findhorn community. It would be unwise for anyone who does not accept this last to work in the Findhorn garden, however competent a gardener he might be otherwise. Disbelief or unacceptance could upset the delicate energy balance in the garden, with undesirable results. Those working in the garden must never forget that there are nature spirits of many kinds working with them; send love to them and give thanks for their cooperation.'

'What about the rest of the community?'

'They must guard against becoming indifferent to the garden. It is so easy for one's environment to become background and unnoticed. Members of the community should develop an awareness of the flowers, bushes and trees as they move about from place to place. They should give thanks to God, the nature spirits and the gardeners for the radiance and vitality in the garden, thus helping to maintain this special garden as something unique and beautiful.'

We spent some time then walking about, circling the trees and bushes or just standing still. In spite of the proximity of a busy street on the other side of a hedge, there was a strange hush, a feeling of being almost on another plane of existence. It had become the focal centre for the nature forces in the Garden; for some particular reason I had to come here with Pan on this day and make an essential contact, though I had often been aware of him there and even seen him previously. The contact made, we left that part of the Garden, going along the path that runs in front of the herbaceous border and then crossing the grass to the beech tree under which I was sitting when the whole thing began in March 1966.

There was no seat beside the tree now, so I stood leaning my back against the trunk, exchanging energies with the tree. The heightened awareness was as strong as ever. I could no longer see Pan but was aware of his presence.

Kurmos appeared in front of the tree where I had first seen him. He was laughing. He danced round the trees just as he had done at that first meeting and then started off in a wide circle round the one I was leaning against, circling it several times, spiralling in towards me until he stopped opposite me and bowed. 'In exalted company today. Am I welcome?'

'You are always welcome.'

I left the tree and started to walk in the direction of the east gate, the one I had entered by, accompanied by the little faun and several elves who had joined us. We went as directly as possible across the Garden to the gate. As Kurmos and I reached it, Pan appeared beside the elves, who were a little behind us, and raised his arm in a farewell greeting.

Kurmos came with me out into the main street.

'Are you coming back to the flat with me?' I asked him. 'You are very welcome.'

'No, I am only seeing you part of the way. This is one of my busy days.'

I grinned at him. 'Is it?'

'Yes it is,' he said gravely. Then he laughed. 'I'm glad I was the first nature spirit you saw.'

'Are you becoming conceited about it?'

'What is conceited?'

'Being pleased with yourself and showing it.'

Kurmos laughed delightedly. 'I am always pleased with myself. Is that wrong?'

'Not in your case. You have every right to be.'

He looked at me with curiosity. 'Aren't you pleased with yourself?'

'Not very often.'

THE FORLORN FAERIE GLEN

'But you ought to be. Existence is so joyful.'

'Only rarely so for human beings.'

He looked downcast. 'But that is sad. I know it's true from the thoughts I pick up and the things I see.'

'I am not unhappy, Kurmos. There is much to rejoice in and from time to time wonderful experiences such as this afternoon in the Garden. I am content but I am not pleased with myself. I fail in so many things.'

He looked astonished. 'I don't believe that. At least you haven't failed in your contacts with Pan and with us. Isn't that something to be pleased about?'

'Yes, Kurmos, it is. I am a privileged person and I know it.'

He smiled. 'That's better. You know that we all love you very much and we will help you as much as we can—all of us.'

'Thank you, Kurmos. That gives me confidence and makes me very happy.'

I felt lighthearted and laughed.

'Now I must go.'

'It is your busy day!'

'Yes, my busy day.' He looked at me, chuckled and, turning, ran back the way we had come, gradually fading out as he did so.

PAN VISITS ROC AT HOME

·

ROC

That evening I wrote up the first part of my account of the day's events, but was unable to finish it as I had an engagement. The following evening I continued the account, sitting in my back room in front of the gas fire. The room was comfortable and quiet. As I wrote Pan sat in the armchair almost opposite me where he had been since I began writing.

'Did all those exchanges actually take place the other day in the Botanics? Or are you giving me more now while I am writing? Am I adding anything myself? It is important to me that it is authentic.'

'Of course it is important it is authentic, as you well know in your own higher being. You are adding nothing. Our exchanges took place in the form of images and symbols as usual. Some of these were not fully realised into words by your mind at the time, but were deeply impressed into your unconscious level and are now being realised into words under my guidance. I am overlighting you during the whole of this transcript. Nothing is being left out and nothing added that should not be there. Personal colouration on your part is kept down to the minimum. When we go through it together later on, if there are any mistakes or wrong transcriptions, I will give you the corrections. Proceed in faith.'

'Thank you for the reassurance. I am always aware of the dangers of false transcription or colouration.'

'Very wise. Now I want to return to your life at Cowford Cottage. I want to be certain that you consciously realise its full significance in your development.'

'What am I not realising? I am well aware of the importance of the close contact with nature.'

'At that time you knew nothing about so-called "power points" and their associated "ley lines"?'

'That is true.'

'Does it surprise you to learn that there was a powerful nature point in the wood behind the outhouses?'

'It certainly does!' I looked at him, startled.

'In spite of your present knowledge and experience of such points it has never occurred to you to think back to your cottage days?'

'No. I suppose knowledge gained at a later date is not always carried back to an earlier time. Behind the outhouses you said. That must have been about the middle of the wood?'

'Yes.' Once more the mischievous twinkle appeared in Pan's eyes. 'It was the exact spot you chose to sunbathe on, and surrounded by the wind breaker you built.'

I must really have looked startled this time. 'Oh no! This is fantastic!'

'It is true. All through the ten years you lived in the cottage, every time you sunbathed you lay naked on the ground on a power point with a thin waterproof sheet between you and the earth. Rubber does not insulate you from these energies.'

'But I felt nothing except a change of energy which I thought was coming from the sun. I knew instinctively it was the right spot to sunbathe on.'

'You were not so sensitive in those days. You were lying in the air on the earth in the sun's rays, and afterwards you bathed in the pool you had made by damming the stream that ran past the cottage. The sun symbolises fire, so you had close and frequent contact with the four "elements" you talk about over a long period. Is it any wonder that you can communicate with the entities that inhabit these elements? During those ten years, all your bodies were being prepared and conditioned by the energies of that power point.'

I was so astonished I could only sit and stare at him.

'Not only was it a nature power point but it was also associated with pre-Christian religious ceremonies and rituals of a druidic nature. Now you understand what I mean when I ask if you fully realise the significance of your stay at the cottage. Also remember it was on a hillock and surrounded by wood.'

I drew a deep breath. 'At the time all I knew was that it was the right place for me.'

'It certainly was. And now I think that is all for the moment.'

When I had finished writing I closed my notebook. Pan had ceased to be visible.

THE WILD GARDEN

·

PETER CADDY

Communication between Roc and the nature spirits at
Findhorn continued regardless of where Roc was, as Peter
Caddy recalls.

Roc's work with the nature spirits also pointed out to us the importance of the wild garden. In Britain, where there is a tradition of fine gardens, almost invariably an area in each is left wild. There is also a folk custom among farmers of leaving a bit of land, where humans are forbidden to go, as the domain of the fairies and elves.

One Sunday afternoon, Roc had accompanied a group of us on a visit to a local walled garden at Kincorth. At one end of the landscaped area ran a stream with a wooden bridge across it. On the other side was a wild place, cool and dense in contrast to the neat and colourful beds on our side. Roc, obeying an impulse, wandered off across the bridge and into the foliage. Later he told us that beyond a certain point in the area he had suddenly felt like an intruder.

There Pan appeared beside him and told him that this part of the garden was for his subjects alone and was to be so respected. He said that in any garden, no matter the size, where the full cooperation of the nature spirits is desired, a part should be left where, as far as possible, man does not enter. The nature spirits use this place as a focal point for their activity, a centre from which to work.

Pan also told him that at Findhorn we did not have enough respect for our wild garden. Indeed, we had developed the habit of crossing this area when we went to the beach for a swim, and right in the middle of it Dennis had set up his tent. You can imagine how quickly he removed both himself and his gear on hearing this message! Thereafter, we made sure to enter this area as seldom as possible.

STRANGE OCCURRENCES
AT FINDHORN

·

DAVID SPANGLER

There were so many facets to Roc's abilities to see further than most. I first met Roc in the fall of 1970 at his flat in Edinburgh. Peter Caddy had driven me down from Findhorn for the occasion, insisting that the two of us had to get together. From what Peter had told me of this man, I certainly had no objections and was anxious to meet him.

I had been in the community myself for less than a month. I had come as a twenty-five-year-old visitor from California, where I had been teaching classes on esotericism and spirituality. From the way Peter had described him and the stories he told me, I was half-expecting a figure out of Tolkien, a modern-day Gandalf. And while Peter was known to exaggerate at times for the sake of a good story, in this case he had not. Roc was everything Peter had said he was and more, a loving man who carried the presence of the invisible worlds with him like a cloak.

Roc lived in a flat at the top of a long flight of stairs (the bathroom was in the other direction, down in the basement). As a book lover with a fairly large library of my own, the first impression I had when he brought Peter and me into his home was of the many bookshelves rising everywhere from floor to ceiling and groaning under the weight of countless volumes of the most fascinating lore. The second thing to catch my eye in his living room was the grand piano, for Roc was an accomplished pianist. And the third aspect I noticed was the sense of a deep, peaceful power in the room. It was like stepping into a temple dedicated to quiet, study and contemplation, a place that was no stranger to the flow of spirit and subtle energies. In the years since, whenever I have imagined what a magician's study might be like, Roc's living room springs to mind.

From things Roc said, I had the impression that he was largely self-trained in the deeper aspects of life. This was an area, though, that he did not discuss with me. He did say that there was a long period when he was younger when he lived a solitary existence in a rural area near an ancient forest, and it was during this time that he came into close contact with the inner worlds. Beyond that he did not elaborate. But, however he gained his knowledge and skill in practice, there was no doubt in my mind—based on my experience of the subtle energies around him—that he was accomplished in this.

The part of his life and work that he did share was his role as a protector. It was certainly known, if not always understood, by most people in the Findhorn community that Roc was an inner guardian of the centre. Part of his work involved creating and maintaining a 'dome' of light and spiritual power around the place for its protection. Although he could and did check on this construct from his flat and at times would send word to Peter if he felt something was amiss, many of his visits to the community were for the purpose of walking about and checking the state of his spiritual wards and protections.

On one such occasion, we were having a run of illnesses in the community. Coincidentally, a healer had arrived and had set up shop, so to speak, in one of the trailers, with Peter's blessing, to work on people. The man himself seemed all right, but over the course of several days, a pattern began to develop that those who had gone to him for healing or just for massages were either getting worse or, if they had not been so before, were actually becoming sick. I was just beginning to investigate this when Roc appeared for one of his visits, saying that he had felt something was wrong in the community. I explained to him what had been going on, and together we went to visit the healer at his trailer.

The healer was not at home, but the trailer was open, so we looked in. As part of his treatment, he had people hold two metal rods to which were attached wires leading out of the trailer to two other rods sunk into the soil a few feet away. Apparently he was using them to attempt to transfer and 'ground' negative energies from his patients into the earth.

Both Roc and I could feel that the subtle energies around the ground where these rods were inserted were chaotic and in turmoil. Roc felt they should be removed, so the two of us walked over to where they were. Roc was a few feet ahead of me, and as I was still walking towards him, he reached down and pulled one of the rods out of the soil. I suddenly felt a flash of energy and a wave of pressure against me, and the next thing I knew I was on my back, looking up at the sky. As I propped myself up, I realised I had been blown back about a foot or so by some force as if an explosion had occurred. I could see that Roc was lying on the ground as well, as if he had been picked up and thrown down two or three feet away from where the rods had been planted.

Obviously pulling out the rod had released a tremendous build-up of subtle energy which had physically lifted both of us up and then knocked us down. We were both unhurt but slightly dazed. One of the rods lay on the ground where Roc had dropped it and the other was still thrust into the earth. Getting to his feet, Roc went over and very carefully pulled it out, but there was no repeat of what had happened before. The build-up of energy had been discharged.

As it turned out, there was an underground stream that none of us had known about, and the healer had inadvertently planted his rods right above it in a way that short-circuited the flow of subtle energies along the course of that stream. This had caused a backup that reversed the flow of energy along his rods and wires, so that rather than discharging negative energies harmlessly from the patient to the earth outside, the exact opposite was happening. This was why most of the people he treated either fell ill or got worse rather than better.

SALAMANDERS, SYLPHS AND UNDINES

·

ROC

*Along with his encounters with Pan, fauns and elves, Roc
also described fascinating meetings with other elementals,
such as the fire and water spirits. His insights into their
existence and function is of much relevance for the healing
of today's world.*

The ancient and medieval philosophers believed all matter was made up of what they called the four elements: earth, air, fire and water. We know today that these are not elements in the chemical sense at all, but they are an important grouping. When we talk about fire, earth, air and water we don't necessarily mean only the physical, because they exist in the etheric realms as well.

These elementals have been given names: fire elementals are called salamanders, the water elementals undines, the air elementals sylphs and the earth elementals gnomes. I extend the name 'elemental' to cover a great number of different beings, belonging and found in those various elements, and it is those beings which I am referring to as belonging to the elemental world.

It is a great pity that humanity has lost contact with this world largely because of materialistic ideas, and lack of belief. The inhabitants of this world can be extremely useful to us, and we are very necessary to them.

I had a scientific training in chemistry, physics and mathematics, and I developed an analytical mind, an observant mind. This I've found has been extremely helpful, because it has made me very cautious in accepting the experiences I've had until I was absolutely certain there was only one explanation for them. Much earlier in life, when I was taking a great interest in what we now call parapsychology, I tried as far as possible to find completely physical explanations for things, and had a tendency, if anything unusual happened, to try to rationalise it.

One person's experience is not necessarily convincing to someone else who hasn't had a similar experience. To me these beings are often quite as solid as any of us. With many of them it is not only a case of seeing them, but of feeling them; I have felt their touch, I have heard their voices. It's a question of all the senses being aware of them.

Whether those senses are heightened varieties of my physical senses or whether other senses come into function here is difficult to differentiate, but I don't think that matters. It is probably a mixture of both.

My first encounter with a fire elemental, a salamander, took place at Findhorn. There were only a few caravans and two bungalows at that time. I was staying by myself in one of the caravans. I want to set the scene by briefly describing the caravan. It was a normal type of caravan with a partition and there were two doors, one leading into the bathroom, the other into a kitchenette. In between the two doors was a fireplace with an anthracite stove in it.

This was not a very big stove; it had great depth but the part that was projecting into the caravan was only one foot by eighteen inches. It was raised off the floor, and round it was a grille made of metal slats. This was about two and a half by three feet in size, and the stove projected about six inches from the middle of it.

It was June, lovely weather, and I'd been there for two or three days. I hadn't lit the stove because I didn't need to. It was about three o'clock in the afternoon and I was writing a letter to a friend, describing a visit we had made the day before to Pluscarden Priory, nine miles from Findhorn. I was halfway down the page when I became aware of what looked like smoke coming through the air spaces between the metal slats. This puzzled me because the stove was not lit; there was no smell of burning or anything. What was this?

I got up, went out of the caravan and looked under the windows, because beneath the stove there was a grating in the floor through which cold air was sucked in. I looked to see if there were any bonfires outside, but there was nothing. I went back into the caravan, sat down, and returned to my letter. Again I saw this vapour, this cloud of smoke coming out of the grille. This time I simply sat and watched.

It got thicker and began to build up until it formed a rough sort of egg shape. Then it grew thicker again, and as it did it began to glow. Its centre was glowing with a most beautiful orange light, and as this happened it began to contract, and gradually a vaguely human shape built up. This was of a very beautiful being about four feet tall, with long waving hair like flame above its head, and all of a beautiful colour. I thought as soon as I saw it: this is a fire salamander.

The being spoke to me. When I say these beings speak to me, the communication is some form of telepathy, and it may well be in ideas, in symbols, which my brain sets into words. When I speak to them, I do actually speak to them, and there seems to be a response. Therefore, when I'm describing this I put it in the form of a dialogue as it appears to me.

This being said to me, 'Do you know what I am?' and I said, 'Yes, you are a fire elemental.'

It came and sat down in the armchair beside the one I was sitting in, and whether I looked uneasy I don't know, but he rather smiled and looked at me and said, 'Don't worry, I won't burn your furniture. I am a cosmic fire salamander and I will not burn anything.' Then he held out his hand and said, 'Give me your hand.'

Again there was a slight hesitation on my part, and he said, 'Oh, are you afraid I'll burn you?' I put out my left hand and he took hold of it.

Now this is a very funny thing, because I could grip his hand, and yet it wasn't entirely solid. All I had was a wonderful feeling of warmth and a tremendous feeling of energy flowing from him. After that he got up and came and stood in front of me. He took hold of me with his two hands, one on each side of my head, and said, 'This is just a preliminary meeting. We will meet again.'

And then he gradually expanded. The glow began to die out, and he became again the smoke, which went back to the slats in the metal. That was my first meeting with a being of that sort.

The next meeting was very strange. This was in Edinburgh. It was a lovely day, and I decided to go down to the Botanic Garden. As I left the front door of my flat and walked along the street, something caught my eye. I turned my head and there seemed to be a flame sitting on my shoulder. I could just see it with difficulty. And then I thought, 'Hello, here is another salamander.'

So I greeted it, and I seemed to hear a rather high piping voice. 'Don't worry, can I come to the Botanic Garden with you?' I walked along and as I turned down into the next street I was aware of a whole lot of little flames on the pavement, running along in front of me. They varied in colour; some were deep red, some were yellow, some a beautiful orange colour.

I asked the little being about their sizes and he said, 'They can be any size they like.' And all the way down to the Botanic Garden I was led by this procession of little flames going down the street. It was a very extraordinary experience indeed.

Since then the first salamander I saw at Findhorn has often come to see me. He is a very strange and beautiful being. Wherever you have a burning fire, you are likely to have those beings. One thing they will do if you believe in them and if you ask them is help you light your fire. The stove I've mentioned at Findhorn is an absolute brute to light. You think it is lit, and then pop, it's out, until I start speaking nicely to it, and say, 'Now, you salamanders help me with this stove, help me to light this fire.' I put a match to it, speak to it again and pop! It would light.

So that was the contact with fire beings.

I have had a number of contacts with water spirits in rivers, in lochs, and in the sea. They are very beautiful beings. When Andrew Glazewski[1] was at Findhorn, I went with him to a most beautiful place called Randolph's Leap. To me this is one of the most enchanted places in this country, because it is a complete fairy centre, and a place for elves and all sorts of beings.

Two rivers join there: the River Findhorn, which is in a deep gorge with very strange rock formations, a very wonderful place, and on the other side the River Divie. On the hill between them is this beautiful glade which is pure fairyland. A number of sensitives who have been there have also seen the elves and fairies, which has given me confirmation that I'm not quite round the bend.

Well, I was there with Andrew and we were walking down the path which is above the river. We stopped and looked down at the beautiful rock formation. Suddenly Andrew said, 'At last I've seen them. Water nymphs!'

They were floating down on the water, and he described very much what I was seeing, which was again a nice confirmation.

Finally to air spirits. They are very strange; sometimes they seem to have wings, sometimes they don't. They seem to be swimming through the air. They are usually slightly transparent, and vary a great deal in colour, and of course in size.

ELVES, FAIRIES AND GOBLINS

·

ROC

The elemental beings have the power to change their size to a quite extraordinary degree.

Sometimes they are very, very tiny, like the little fairy beings you get inside the blossoms of flowers. There are very often tiny little elves or fairies in the blossoms of the flowers and this is why, if you have to pull plants or flowers up, or cut them, it shouldn't be done when they're in bloom. As we know at Findhorn, it must never be done to broom or gorse when it is in bloom because those are magical plants and the results can be rather bad.

One day in Edinburgh I felt that something had gone wrong at Findhorn. I rang up Peter Caddy that night and said, 'What on earth have you been doing?'

He said, 'What do you mean?'

'You've done something in the garden. What is it?'

He said, 'I haven't been doing anything.'

Well, it turned out there was a gorse bush which had slightly overgrown a pear tree, and Peter was afraid the pear tree would be choked. He asked one of the boys to cut down part of it. It was in full bloom, and this boy was very reluctant because he was a great lover of nature and believed in nature spirits. He thought he

MAGIC ON MIDSUMMER EVE

was doing the wrong thing and was almost weeping while he did it, apologising all the time.

This was what was wrong, and when I went to Findhorn shortly afterwards I found that a lot of the broom elves and some of the other nature spirits had left the garden. On my way down to the beach, which covered a moor where there were masses of the broom and gorse all in full bloom, I was aware of the tiny little beings in the blossoms. As I was walking along, three beautiful little elves, whom I knew to be broom elves, started walking with me. What they wanted to know was why that bush had been cut down. So I had to explain to them that it was done in ignorance, and that they must be very tolerant with humans, because we very often do things of this sort out of sheer ignorance. So they went back to the garden.

The pear tree died soon after in any case, so it was not saved by cutting the bush back. Shortly after that, broom was growing too vigorously around some blackcurrant bushes and it looked as if they too might be choked. So I was asked by Peter, 'Can I cut down this broom? This is a matter of food. We need the berries. If the bushes die this is going to deprive us of food. Surely this is all right.'

I had a very strong impulse to tell him, 'You know, if you think it is worth cutting the broom bushes, in view of what you know, go and do it, and see what happens.'

He said, 'If you put it like that, I can't.' He left it. It was a very bad year for blackcurrants all around the district, yet those bushes had a heavier yield of fruit than they had ever had before, more than anyone else had. Baskets full of blackcurrants came off the bushes.

You see, these nature beings have infinite power. There is very little they can't do. It is quite easy for them to prevent the broom choking the blackcurrants. This we have got to learn. I'll come a bit later to the full cooperation we must try to achieve between those spirits and others, but there are one or two other things I'd like to tell you first.

I found out a very interesting thing: those broom elves were yellow, the colour of broom blossom, and they seemed to have little hats on their heads, in the shape of the blossom. Of course, those elemental beings don't wear clothes in the way we do. What appear to be clothes are part of themselves; what you could call a part of their aura. Rather to my surprise, although

I might have expected it, I found the broom elves turned entirely green in the winter—which is also the colour of broom in winter. Other times I have been aware of heather elves, which are a most beautiful purple colour.

I had the most extraordinary experience on the beach once. When I was walking along I was joined by a number of . . . I suppose I could only call them a kind of goblin, although they were not black, not evil. They were the most incredible looking beings: a yellow sandy colour, with totally round bodies, round heads and very thin legs and arms. They had rather bulging eyes, with huge ears on the top of their heads, like rabbits. They were the most delightful and merry beings, turning somersaults, running about and laughing. One of them actually climbed up and sat on my shoulder.

Quite often I've seen these little beings when they are on the beach; one incident rather amused me. As I was going along the beach, a couple of people were coming behind me whom I didn't quite like the feel of. I thought there was an aggressiveness, something unpleasant about them, and I had a feeling I wanted to be alone on the beach.

Now there is a question whether I was right to do this or not, because one shouldn't do things for one's own self, but I thought, 'Why should those people be following me like that?' And I said to the little goblins who were there, 'Can't you do something about it? I think they have walked far enough along the beach; turn them back.' The whole lot ran off, all laughing and making a noise down the beach, and I walked on without looking back for a while. Then I turned round and behold—the couple were walking back the other way, and all those little beings were coming running after me absolutely full of delight!

It is important to try to find out what the elementals really are like, what they are, and why they take the form they do. They have two forms, one basic and one a body of light. I feel I'm very lucky because I am able to see this light body, and it is incredibly beautiful; a whirl of energy, rather like a nebula. It is very, very transparent and beautifully coloured, maybe a number of colours, or one colour. And it has an extraordinary appearance of fine lines which are in constant motion, which seem to be flowing almost like fluid through a pipe, always curved; all the time interweaving, forming the most exquisite patterns, and their colours are wonderful. It would be almost impossible for an artist, however clever he was, to depict them, because our colours are not pure enough.

Now this is the form of most of those elementals in their original state. To the best of my belief they are part of what is known as the angelic hierarchy, probably the part of the hierarchy which is nearest to earth. They are all servants of God, and work under God's will.

I believe that what we call the devas, the great angelic beings, are the architects; the beings who design the archetypal form that any plant or tree or fruit, anything of the vegetable kingdom, is going to take, and they channel down cosmic energies. The nature spirits are the builders. They work with this blueprint of the deva, and build up what is really the etheric counterpart, what Reshad Feild[1] called body number one. It is within this that the physical tree grows up.

Most people would say all you have to do is plant the seed and the tree will grow, because the whole pattern of the tree is contained in the genetic code, in the DNA molecule in the seed. I am more and more coming to believe that the DNA molecule itself has an etheric counterpart, which may well have little elemental beings working in it, and I wonder if it could replicate itself without this. In fact, I wonder if any vegetable form would grow if it had not the help of these beings.

Elementals cannot work within this etheric counterpart in their light body; they have to take on an etheric body to do this. Where do they get this? Very largely from us, from humanity. You see, in all myths and legends are supernatural beings, like fairies or gods. Myths, with their constant repetitions, have built up the concept of such ideas. They have, if you like, made a thought form which these beings can take on in order to work with the trees, the plants and so on.

Also, the elementals know that since those legends have been written, humanity should be able to recognise them (though, as modern man dismisses fairytales as a lot of childish nonsense, they are not always identified). This is why Pan appears in the form he does, because he was best known in the myths of Greece as half human and half animal. He is very insistent that he is accepted in this form, because humanity has given it to him, and therefore must accept him like this.

This, as I've said before, is a very symbolic form; the human upper half represents the human intelligence and aspirations, and the animal lower half represents very deep nature forces which are not present in a human being at all. Some people have suggested that Pan is very ugly, because the picture they seem to get of this being is one they think ugly. This is absolutely untrue; Pan is one of the most beautiful beings I've ever seen. One has to learn to judge these beings in their own right, and not compare them with humanity. In our conceit we seem to think ours is the perfect form, and therefore anything that is at all approaching human must be like us or it is ugly. This idea changes when we get to know those beings.

INSIGHTS INTO THE
ELEMENTAL KINGDOM

•

ROC

One afternoon I was in the Botanic Garden, sitting in a seat, watching a lot of little gnomes. They were playing about underneath a tree, and I thought to myself, 'Yes, they look like a lot of delightful, fat little babies.' One of them pricked up his ears, turned around, looked at me in annoyance, came stalking over, put his hands on his hips and said, 'I am not fat!'

A lot of them seem to behave in a very human manner. Along with the form which has been put onto them by humanity, humanity has also put a good deal of human behaviour on them. In the writing of our fairy stories and myths, we have tended to give the gods, the spirits and the elves considerable human attributes, and therefore they tend to take this on with the form, which explains why they sometimes behave in a human manner.

It is easy to think of a tiny little fairy or gnome who is working away, 'Oh yes, that's a nice little creature, but of course it hasn't got much power.' We have got to realise that however tiny, however filmy, however unreal these beings may seem, they have got infinite power. Even the tiniest little fairy has enormous power.

The elemental kingdom is a totally different evolution. It may be they evolve just as humanity does, but

I believe, and this has largely come from what these beings have told me themselves and from what I have conjectured from my various encounters with them, that the elementals existed long before humanity did. They are not beings particularly associated with this planet; they are cosmic beings. They existed before the earth and were certainly present on the earth long before us. We might therefore say at one time the elementals were the lords of earth until the creation and appearance of humanity.

Humanity is different because we have been incarnated in order to experience self-consciousness, in order to have a degree of self-will, of free will, in order to develop. Humanity therefore was given authority over the elementals, and over the animal kingdom, but it has most horribly abused that authority!

The elementals say, 'All right, humanity has authority, but if it misuses that authority, we are not compelled to obey it.' If they felt it was right, they could even withdraw completely. In fact, under certain circumstances they would do this, because they couldn't do anything else.

You see, humanity has complete authority over the earth; it can do with it what it likes, and unfortunately, because of our short-sighted policies and our greed, we are doing our best to destroy it. Of course this is a matter of great concern to the elementals. Even if we blow the earth to bits, they will still exist, because they will just go back to their other form on a totally different dimension, but what humanity is doing does concern them, to the extent that a great many of them, at times, are very hostile to mankind. They feel humanity is a parasite on the face of the earth: 'Look what he is doing to it!'

We mustn't entirely look on the dark side, because humanity has done some wonderful work. We have created very great beauty in buildings and landscaping, but at the same time we have done an awful lot of harm. We are becoming very aware nowadays of what humanity is doing in the way of pollution, pouring so much filth into the waters of the earth, into the atmosphere, into the earth itself. If we want to do that we can do it, but you see, we are going to destroy ourselves if we go on doing it. It is a very, very good thing that nowadays humanity is waking up to this, but we must realise these dangers and try to counter them before we reach the point of no return.

This is where the elementals can be of tremendous help. These beings will help anybody who believes in them, who is prepared to send them love, and who asks for their help in their garden, as long as they are not doing things elementals dislike, like using artificial fertilisers or insecticides, or mutilating flowers too much in order to get bigger blooms. As I said, they have infinite power. They have total control over growth. A time could come when they would produce what humanity wants.

Humanity may start to believe in them, but it must never feel it is their superior and that they are its servants. Nor are they superior to humanity. Whatever collaboration comes about must be absolutely *not* one sided, but in complete balance between the two. Humanity is inclined to think, 'I am the lord of the earth, and what I want to do I *will* do. If I want to cut the forest down I shall do it, and I don't care what harm it does to the animals, or to the elementals, and I don't believe in *them* in any case.' Humanity has got to come to the point where it has respect for the animal kingdom, for the elemental kingdoms, for the devic kingdoms, because the whole lot should be able to live in peace and harmony, with complete cooperation.

Some of those beings find it very difficult to understand human behaviour. 'Why is it that here we have a race of beings who simply talk about love, about brotherhood, but cannot live together? They are constantly fighting, constantly killing each other. We never do that. What's wrong with mankind?'

One can quite understand their extreme puzzlement over this human behaviour. Yet they are quite infinitely tolerant. You see, they could cause terrible disasters. In fact, if they withdrew from the earth, although you would get growth, and would get vegetables and fruits growing, they would have no life force in them. It is doubtful how much good they would be. When I first met the little faun, one of the things he told me is that the nature forces were getting rather tired of humanity. He said, 'If you think you can get on without us, just try.' And this is very true.

This is why it is important to revive a belief in these beings so we can get full cooperation from them, not only from the earth spirits but from the others. One of the functions of the water spirits, for example, is to purify water. There is so much filth in so many rivers and lakes nowadays that they won't try to do it; they are not going to do it unless humanity stops polluting and asks for their help. But they could do it; if you believe in them, they could help enormously to clean up the mess. The same goes for the air spirits; they could help tremendously in cleansing the atmosphere, because this is one of their functions.

The fire elementals have another function. There is not only physical, material pollution, there is spiritual and mental pollution. There is so much hatred, envy and greed that there are a tremendous lot of bad thought forms being built up. Thought has a tremendous power of remaining; it can remain as a thought form. Wherever you have got strife on the earth, you will get thought forms being attracted and helping to fan the flames, to build it up. One of the functions of the fire spirits is to clean away these wrong thought forms. These thought forms make up part of the etheric shell of the earth. Fire spirits can purify this. They can disperse wrong thought forms, and therefore their help would be very, very useful.

THE QUESTION OF EVIL

·

ROC

I said I believed the elementals were part of the angelic hierarchy. Some people have often said, and this is something I have to touch on, that there are no bad nature spirits, there are no evil beings. But of course there are. I do not class them as true elementals, but they exist. There are several kinds. Again we have the possibility of humanity building up thought forms. We may do it by simply thinking evil thoughts. We could also do it, I believe, by writing. We could create such things as vampires: thought forms which could be activated by some sort of negative energy, and then you would get black goblins. I know this because I have seen them. I have on several occasions had to deal with them.

I've been in places where there is a terrible feeling of darkness, where the nature spirits—I will call them that—are of this black nature. In one garden I visited, the owner said, 'I'd like you to have a look at this apple tree because I'm not happy about it. I get a horrible feeling from it.' As soon as I approached the tree, I saw black beings working round the base of the trunk. This tree was evil.

The lady asked me, 'What am I to do? Shall I get it cut down?' I said yes.

Her idea was that it would be best burned, but a local wood carver asked her if he might have the wood of the trunk of the tree in order to make carvings out of it. She was very worried about this. However, she decided to let him have it. He was unable to use the wood because the tree had long nails driven into it all down the trunk. There was an old custom, which belongs to witchcraft, of driving a nail into a tree with a curse on it, with a name attached to the nail, and this was apparently what had happened in the case of this tree. This would explain why there was darkness there.

So certain places have such beings that need to be cleansed, though they are not lost beings because something interesting can happen. One of the rivers at Randolph's Leap, the Divie, was oddly enough on the dark side. The River Findhorn was a place of light, but the Divie was a place of strange darkness; apparently, a long time ago, the area was inhabited by people who were nature lovers, and lived in huts and caves. Then a tribe came along who were not good and killed them all. This tribe went in for human sacrifices which they flung over into the Divie. This gave it its bad character, and on many occasions I was aware of very nasty black beings crawling about on the river bank.

One time when I was visiting there I was inspired. I was directed from within to carry out a form of exorcism to try to get rid of them, and disperse them, in which they were given a choice of either coming over to the Light or being banished to outer darkness. This had to be done several times, and apparently it was effective because the dark has gone from that side.

Not long ago I went to Randolph's Leap, and walking up the path in front of me by the side of the Divie were three very beautiful green elves. When we got to the top, I realised those were three of the dark goblins who had chosen to come over to the Light, and had been transmuted. So this can happen.

I have said that it is the fairy stories, the legends, that have given the elemental beings the form in which they appear. Incidentally, the same goes for the Greek and Norse gods: they actually can appear. We can, if you like, regard those elementals as forces, energies, because that is what they are. So, just as the particles forming the atom may not be matter at all, but consist of whirls of energy, these beings are really energy, an intelligent energy, which can become personalised.

The great modern myth is *The Lord of the Rings* by J.R.R. Tolkien. It is my belief that because this book is so popular and is being read so much, we will begin to get some elementals taking on the forms in Tolkien's book. In fact, the elves I'm seeing nowadays are remarkably like those of Tolkien. Now this could be because reading Tolkien has produced a picture in my mind, and I am projecting a form and therefore they appear to me like that.

I have been told these beings will appear to people very much as a person expects to see them. If a person expects to see an angel in long white robes with wings, wearing a halo and carrying a harp, then that is how he will see it. I probably have remains of fairytales from youth that might govern the way I see these beings.

MEETING NATURE SPIRITS

·

ROC

*Over the years, many people asked Roc how he came to
see nature spirits. Brian Nobbs remembers Roc telling
him, 'It seems to be necessary to have reached some level
of cosmic consciousness before you can experience nature
spirits directly.' While this may seem very complex, Roc
seems to suggest it need not be so—that it is dependent
on opening up to nature with love, discernment and respect.
As far as his own story is concerned, Roc discovered that the
seeds of his remarkable experiences were clearly sown in
early childhood.*

On one of my visits to Findhorn, I went with Paul Hawken to Rosemarkie, a little seaside town on the north shore of the Moray Firth. I had been taken there by my parents during the Easter vacation in 1903 when I was approaching my fourth birthday.

There was an enchanting place there known as the Faerie Glen which I loved and was taken to several times. It was then part of a large estate and was well preserved. I have always had vivid memories of those early visits: of a waterfall with two streams of water, a flight of earthen steps, a bridge over a stream, and above all a wishing well under an overhanging rock with a pebbly bottom into which I used to drop a penny while making a wish.

The estate was broken up a long time ago and the glen has gone wild and natural. The trees are of course different since that visit seventy years ago. They are new trees that have grown up since then. Some stumps remain of much older ones. Paul and I went right up to the head of the glen where we found the bridge over the stream and the new flight of steps, which were built fairly recently.

I found where the wishing well had been under the overhanging rock; it was now completely filled in.

And we came upon the waterfall, splashing down into a rocky pool. It was a lovely day and we sat on rocks, looking at the falling water and enjoying the feel of the place.

Suddenly three little gnomes appeared on a flat rock in front of me. 'My, you have grown up,' said one of them.

'What do you mean?'

'We remember a little boy coming here long ago in your time,' piped in the second gnome.

'Aren't you glad your wish was granted?' asked the third.

'What wish?'

'Don't you remember dropping a penny in the wishing well and wishing you could see fairies and talk with them?' the first gnome asked.

'And bubbles rose from the pebbles at the bottom of the well, which meant that your wish would be granted,' added the second.

I certainly did drop pennies in the well and made wishes. I cannot say I remember that specific one but it is very likely true, as I believed in fairies then as I do once more today. So that could be how it all began and why it happened to me.

To anyone who may have expressed a wish to see and talk to nature spirits, whether or not they dropped a penny into a wishing well, remember it took sixty-three years for my wish to be granted—so don't lose hope.

THE END

If Merlin's owl lighted on his shoulder, you would
hardly be surprised.

PAUL HAWKEN, *THE MAGIC OF FINDHORN*, P. 203

AFTERWORD

My experiences with nature and Roc

·

CO-FOUNDER OF FINDHORN, DOROTHY MACLEAN

*While Roc was having his experiences with the nature spirits,
Dorothy Maclean had made contact with the devas, the
powerful beings of light who oversee the wellbeing of each
species on the planet. These encounters, detailed in her book
To Hear the Angels Sing, were to forever change our
understanding of living nature. Through the wisdom the
devas shared came the miracle of the Findhorn garden.*

BEGINNINGS

My own connections with nature began with my searching
into the purpose of life and discovering that all world
religions agreed that God (which to me is the life force
in anyone and everything) is love. Through learning to
love, humans can therefore become conscious of their
divinity. This became my faith.

Then I had a difficult test: was I willing to follow the
loving way although it meant going against my greatest
personal desire? After months of struggling to do this, I
had a cosmic experience of knowing and being part of my
inner divinity. This changed me completely; my friends
said that it even changed my voice. Soon after, a thought
kept coming to me, asking me to 'stop, listen and write'.
In spite of my doubts I eventually did just that, and for
almost ten years received wonderful teachings from God
three times a day. Peter and Eileen Caddy had also begun
to turn within, and we each developed our own unique
inner contact, finding that no matter what situation came
up, we could find help and resolution for it.

Then we arrived at a windswept caravan park at
Findhorn, could not find any jobs and went on national
assistance. To augment our diet, Peter began to grow

vegetables on the sandy, pebbly soil there. The vegetables produced were very sickly. One morning I received that I had a job to feel into the forces of nature. I was told that I could cooperate with them in the garden and to begin by tuning into the higher overlighting nature spirits, the spirits of differing physical forms such as clouds, rain, vegetables. I was told they would be overjoyed to find some humans eager for their help. These beings are of the Light, willing to help but wary of humanity's actions at present. Eventually I chose to attune to my favourite vegetable, the garden pea. Contact was made, and I received that humans were powerhouses who by using their innate faculties could work with the nature spirits. I had no word for these beings, who to me were formless energy fields, and so had to use limiting expressions like angel or deva.

The devas answered Peter's questions specifically, such as how far apart to plant seeds, but never ordered us to do anything as they wanted us to work with them as equals from our inner divinity. They were delighted that Peter followed their suggestions in the garden. Peter, of course, would first try to find a reason for a plant's malfunction himself, but when he found none or did not know what to do, he would give me questions. Then I would attune to the spirit of the particular vegetable for the answer. For instance, we had two sowings of dwarf beans; the first didn't come up while the second lot seemed promising. The spirit essence of dwarf beans told me that the first lot had been sown too deeply and before the soil had sufficient nutrition, but the other was fine and was being worked on by them. The spinach sprouted so well that Peter asked if it was too thick and I received: 'If you want strong natural growth of the leaf, the plants will have to be wider apart than they are at the moment. By leaving them as they are you will get as much bulk in the leaves, they will perhaps be a little more tender but with not as strong a life force. I of course like to see the plants given full scope, but the choice is up to you.'

COOPERATION WITH NATURE

The devas communicated a vital urgency about this cooperation, seeing it as an evolutionary shift for humanity necessary for the fitness of our world, as we could destroy the planet unless we changed our habits. Also, partnering with them was bringing to human consciousness the fact that nature and humans are both part of the divine

Oneness of life. I was helped to understand this by inner guidance: 'In your research you come across what are called cosmic influences on the earth emanating from the various planets. Think of that planet as a living Being, and also as the forces being relayed by Beings and being received by Beings. There is no such thing as dead matter. Everything is living and everything has a place in My one life; and that life force is more than what you call magnetism. It is an influence consciously wielded on the higher levels. You are simply surrounded by life; you are a life force moving among other life forces. As you recognise this and open up to them, you draw near to them and become one with them, and work with them in My purposes.'

By the time I met Roc in the mid 1960s, the Findhorn garden was flourishing and proving that co-creating with the intelligence of nature brought valid results. Over and over again, we learnt that when we trusted in working with love, miracles happened. Over time other people joined us in this work and we became a community—much to our surprise, for we had had no plans for that to happen and simply relied on inner guidance for our actions in the moment. The devas communicated a great deal, such as the following: 'We come to your consciousness in the joy of our worlds and wonder anew at the complications human beings make with their minds. As contact with us always uplifts you, so it is with all members of the nature kingdom. There is no evil in our worlds; your so-called evil only enters in with human consciousness and interference. It may seem that some elementals are very strange and even hostile, but then so do some races of human beings seem very strange to you, and it is simply that they are different.

'A New Age dawns, an era when all this misunderstanding and hostility falls away like mist in the sun, when all God's creation walk in the Light and in joy together, loving one another, understanding one another and praising God. Hold this in your consciousness. Do not think negatively.

'The nature kingdom needs its champions to help redress the balance that has been upset by humans, but it is balance that needs to be found and balance is not a position of rigidity, but one of great ease, a flowing with every movement, of non-resistance, of giving and taking and adjusting, of forever seeking Oneness, of being close to the Creator. In the wholeness of creation all life serves and complements each other. The nature kingdom offers its abundance as long as humans obey universal law. Humans do need to change and are changing, as we rejoice to see.

'Come share our gaiety, you solemn humans! Life is wonderful! Just be what you truly are, and find Oneness with all.'

MORE ABOUT ROC

Roc was drawn to the work we were doing in cooperation with nature, and of course his story of meeting the faun in the Edinburgh Botanic Garden endeared him to all of us. I was immediately drawn to him, although he was a reserved person and not outgoing in spite of the twinkle of fun in his eyes. He had a presence, seeming to be a magician, a Merlin figure, and he fitted right into the community whenever he came—and he came almost every weekend. I very much enjoyed his company, and he seemed to agree with my views. I did not know his history; his quiet reticence kept him from sharing his personal life and history and my own shy reserve kept me from asking him, so though he spent time with us all, we never really felt that we knew him well.

His nature spirit contact enlarged our perspective on cooperation with nature, for until he arrived we did not take into account the function of the elementals, who are the form builders of nature. They represent the energy of earth, air, fire and water and have long been contacting humans, who have given them forms according to their connection to earth (goblin, gnome); air (fairy, sylph); fire (salamander); and water (undine, sea spirit, nereid). Throughout the world and in most cultures, the elementals have been recognised and given form, often depicted in the garb of an era, such as medieval times, when many people were aware of them. Nowadays they are considered as mythological figures, or superstitious nonsense, and few recognise their reality.

The nature experiment that we were engaged in is to me the second planetary job given to us; the first is to communicate widely the fact that everyone can make conscious contact with their inner divinity, and the second that people can communicate and co-create with the inner intelligence of nature. I was given help from God in the connection: 'Meet and mingle with these beings. More than a few thoughts exchanged are contained in our contact; it is an exchange and a beginning of a unique and far-reaching cooperation. They are amazed and delighted that their cooperation is sought and then followed so faithfully, especially at this time in the world's evolution when man is increasingly harming their work. It is not only important but vital that a new relationship be established, and you are pioneering in this. Give everlasting thanks for My plans, and believe in Me.'

NATURE SPIRITS

As I said in the beginning, in my work with the devas I had always experienced them as formless fields of energy. I discussed with Roc the formlessness of the beings I contacted, and he completely agreed, saying that the nature spirits that he encountered were formless and that we humans were the ones who had endowed them with form through our imaginations. I believe humanity finds it difficult to communicate with formlessness and therefore automatically 'sees' form, particularly as there are similar stories all over the world of gnomes, fairies, sylphs, salamanders, and other nature forms and beings.

When Roc talked about his connection with nature beings, his imagination was clothing these entities in images arising from the many planetary cultures which have existed on earth for thousands of years, in this case images from Greek mythology. These are our interpretations of the energies of nature, of earth, air, fire and water, which have been and are held by humans everywhere in forms that every culture had produced, interpreted, changed, depicted, represented and portrayed in connection with the beings of nature. That is, he was picking up thought forms already existing within the collective consciousness of humanity. Having thought forms made it easier for us to connect with that which is formless. However, Roc knew that it is important for us to not limit these beings to any form, that to do so was to lose real understanding of what the beings represented. They are vaster than any shape can hold.

Because the elementals hold the energies of earth, air, water and fire, we have denoted them accordingly in our imaginations by having an earth being with, say, a pickaxe, or an air being with wings, or a water being swimming, or a fire being as a flaming salamander. We have come to believe that our imagined forms are real. According to Roc, the elementals know of our misunderstandings and have even sometimes taken on such forms to help us communicate with them. I remember being told that once a thought springs into human consciousness, it then percolates around and is picked up elsewhere. It is not surprising that when we contact nature beings, we see them in these imagined forms.

I received the following helpful message about nature spirits early on: 'The nature spirits and the spirits of the elements do not have a birth, lifespan and death as humans do; they simply arise to meet a need, to fulfil a function, to set about a purpose. Take the wind, for example, or a fire; when the life forces that comprise these elements are strong enough and there is wind or fire, the spirits of the wind or the fire are there, present, born in that instant, to vanish from whence they came in the next instant. The spirits of the plants come out of the great store of life force for a purpose and return to it when their purpose is achieved.

'This makes our role sound a very workaday one, only in existence for a purpose. That is so and yet it is not so in the normal human meaning, for our work is our play. Our forces are vividly channelled in the present, and we are, forever, in the present. Even when we are not in manifestation, we are in the great stream of life force to some purpose. Our Creator and your Creator can quite easily, always, find a purpose for us, because life is meant to be enjoyed, to be lived. Now, we go back from whence we came, leaving this thought with you.'

I discovered that Roc and I, in our dealings with nature, often did not agree with Peter's approach. Based on his Rosicrucian training, Peter believed that it was man's job to give direction to the nature spirits, while I believed that our job was to learn to cooperate. We agreed that love was a key, and for me asking about and respecting their natural ways was important. Peter would not always listen to me—certainly I was mouse-like and lacked self-esteem at that time—but in his respect for Roc, Peter always paid attention to his point of view. This often caused me to get Roc to present to Peter his view, which was the same as mine, because Peter would accept from him what he would not from me.

ROC'S ASSISTANCE

At times Roc would be contacted by the nature spirits about something we humans at Findhorn were doing in our work in the garden that was upsetting to them. For instance, one day when Peter was trimming some garden bushes that were in bloom, Roc phoned to ask what we were doing, as the nature spirits came to him in a disturbed state. Apparently trimming plants while they are blooming disrupts the flow of energy. From this we learned not to cut back plants while they are in flower and growing, but when the plant growth is more quiescent. This is the kind of sensitivity Roc added to my own, and together we got through to Peter.

Here is another example: Peter wanted long stems for a good arrangement of sweet peas and followed the usual gardener's approach to this by pinching off the young flower buds. Roc and I both mentioned our dislike of this practice, it being unnatural and invasive, but in this case Peter ignored even Roc. I attuned to the sweet pea deva, and received: 'I come in like a breath of our perfume, fresh and clear-coloured, gay and dainty, not the promise but the fulfilment of the perfection of sweet pea beauty and above the world of error.

'Still I wonder that you ask why flowers do not naturally have long stems. Long stems have been forced by humans by distorting the natural growth and creating a mutilated, unbalanced plant. This is the sort of treatment which causes our kingdom to distrust and move away from humans. You have dominion on earth, and there is nothing we can do about your treatment when you consider only your own ends regardless of means. But you cannot expect us, particularly those who direct the production of each plant, to feel drawn to humans who do not permit us the freedom to enjoy unfolding the perfect pattern.

'The answer to this problem lies in cooperation, in working together for and with the plan of the whole. You wish long stems in order to arrange the flowers in large groups. This can be done when all concerned are working for the project. It cannot be done by outer destruction of part of the plant but by inner concentration on the desired development by all concerned. You humans have a large part to play in this because you are the innovators of change. To ensure our cooperation you have to make clear to and convince our various members that what you are asking is purely motivated and for the good of the whole. Then you must ask, believing, really believing. It should not be an experiment just for the sake of experiment, but always for a useful productive end, part of the great forward movement of life. You wonder how to know when we are convinced. Our kingdom is not unreasonable, but some members are justifiably suspicious. Therefore it would be wise to go softly until you are proved trustworthy.

'With full cooperation between our kingdoms, developments are beyond imagination. We on the devic level would hold a blueprint for that time when all creation is working together under God for the good of all, and there is life-giving harmony between us. We will play our part. Will you play yours?'

I do not have copies of any message that Roc might have received on this subject, but he did agree with what I got. Another part of Roc's overall work, he told me, was to re-energise power points throughout the planet. For this purpose he often made trips, usually with Peter, to various places not only in Britain but elsewhere. He would stand on the particular power point and concentrate inwardly. I don't know exactly what he did, as he never said; I would just see him standing there.

THE QUESTION OF GOOD AND EVIL

Another aspect of his work was to deal with good and evil; neither Eileen nor I had any involvement in this, and we just ignored that subject at the time. I assume he was neutralising an unbalance. None of us know what his main role was. I do remember that he said he put a 'protective shield' over the community, which was designed to keep out negative energies. One day we got a call from Roc asking what was going on up at Findhorn as someone was tearing holes in the shield. We discovered that one of the visitors had seen what he perceived as a block to the energies and a whole lot of beings trapped outside trying to get in, so he, the visitor, removed the block to let them come in. While in Edinburgh, Roc was aware of this action and alerted Peter who asked the visitor to stop what he was doing, explaining that the shield was there for a purpose. I also believe that Roc acted as a protector to Britain as a whole.

THE GIFT OF NATURE SPIRITS

Roc evidently considered it important, even vital, to recognise the power of the elementals, for unless we do this by harmonising and co-creating with them, we can destroy our planet. Our failure to recognise the truth that nature is part of the whole, instead of us humans completely dominating the planet by our choices, leads to the destruction or ruin of world patterns through consequences such as global warming.

Roc's stories of the nature beings are a first step towards working with them. I have sometimes wondered why Roc told his stories in terms of visual images. Yet, I have myself experienced giving form to various entities. When I first encountered the personality aspects of a city, I automatically and mentally gave them a human form. It was the natural thing to do, although it took me some time to realise that it was my own imagination that was moulding them. We all do it, like calling the United States 'Uncle Sam'.

In the Christian world, Pan is portrayed as being a creature of evil. Nature beings, however, are above polarity, above the opposites and containing all qualities, so we humans do not normally perceive them. We have been trained and educated to automatically judge all opposite qualities as either good or evil, positive or negative, and therefore do not consider another possibility. Perhaps because of our almost instinctive beliefs in this area, Roc chose to use images like that of Pan as a way to expand our awareness beyond polarity.

To Roc, Pan was his close ally. In Grecian myth, Pan is a fairly lowly god, the god of the woodlands, feared by those who pass the woods at night, leading to a panic terror. Although from a different derivation, 'pan' also has the connotation of 'all' and is often used in that context: pan-Hellenic, pantheon, pantheistic, panorama, panoptic. Roc generally used the word Pan in its meaning of 'allness'.

At Findhorn I found, amongst the many acres of gorse that almost surrounded our community, a little grove carpeted by exquisite little wildflowers. I often went there to find peace and harmony in nature and away from people. When I once took Roc there, he said that this was Pan's headquarters in the area. This delighted me deeply!

Roc often said he did not want his work to be seen as a contact with cutesy and delightful fairies, for what he contacted were vastly powerful beings. Also, he asked that no one try to portray Pan in picture form, for no one could possibly convey the power of that being. Roc wanted no glamour attached to what he did, and he was very clear in emphasising these subjects.

Imagination is a faculty we use greatly in our contact with different realms and it is certainly used when we 'see' nature spirits. Although it is an important conduit for understanding different or unknown dimensions, it is open to misuse. With imagination we can perceive different realities and invent, perceptualise, conjure up, dream, nurture, create, devise, guess, presume, et cetera.

It is a wonderful tool, one too often not valued. At the same time, we can let our imagination run away with us and lead us into matters so ungrounded that we get lost not only in whimsy but in realms that become so real to us that we get stuck in them. Or we might develop spiritual pride, like people who, because they think they 'see' fairies, consider themselves special and highly developed.

LOOKING TO THE FUTURE

But it is not our imagination that the world is in a dangerous state. In the current difficult times, it is hard to know how we can help the situation. Developing our inner contact is something we can do. We are in fact divine beings who have the faculties for changing ourselves and our environment. We can pray for the highest and best in any situation, and in so doing put our deepest love and intent into it. This is an energy exchange. Our aim is to do everything with that love. I cannot emphasise enough how powerful our divine love energy is. Wielded with passion this force can move worlds. We don't know what the highest and best is, but the universe knows and responds to our asking. Ask and ye shall receive. We make it a powerful energy exchange when we give all our love and passion to bring God's will to the moment.

Let us be aware of our mistaken beliefs, so that we can attune to the wonderful energies of nature without limiting them to any particular form. If we do that, we can truly blend our energies with theirs, for we humans have the capacities in our God-selves to attune to whatever lives on the planet. It is vital at this time, when so much of humanity is polarised to the greed of the lower levels, for us to be open to truth, to vital natural energies and to the harmony needed to save the planet. Let us cease glamorising form and instead ground the reality. Let us bring together the many mansions on this earth.

Remembrances of Roc

·

DAVID SPANGLER

I was always amazed that when Roc visited the Findhorn community, he went swimming in the waters of the Moray Firth even on the coldest days of winter—a truly heroic deed as far as I was concerned, coming as I did from warm California. Roc wore different hats when he came to Findhorn to visit. The one that most people saw was that of the clairvoyant older gentleman who had met Pan and worked with the nature spirits. Roc felt that he had been charged with the job of heightening public awareness of the existence and work of the nature spirits and that meant sharing his story of meeting the faun in the Royal Botanic Garden at Edinburgh and his tales of his encounters with Pan.

This was not an easy task for him, given a shyness and reticence in his nature. But he felt keenly the importance of Findhorn's mission to bring the awareness of the intelligence of nature back into the consciousness of modern men and women. He knew that the problems humanity was creating in its interactions with the earth would only get worse until we learned how to lovingly cooperate with all the visible and invisible kingdoms of life that share this planet with us. He had been given a part to contribute in helping this to come about and he was dedicated to carrying it through.

He was also concerned that his experiences with Pan and the other nature spirits might lead people to feel that was the only way they could be seen or known. Roc himself saw them in other ways as well, often as beings of light without a recognisable form—which was how I generally saw them myself. But he knew Pan had appeared to him as he did in the classical Greek form of half man, half animal for a reason. It was to emphasise the unity of humanity with nature and our need to accept ourselves as part of a larger continuum of life in this world. Here the form was part of the message itself. Certainly, as physical creatures, we respond to concrete images more powerfully and viscerally than we do to pure abstractions and formlessness. The image of Pan as a giant faun is dramatic and meaningful. It stays with a person and can inspire possible further investigation and inspiration. I might talk about Pan, as I have done, as something akin to a sparkling cloud of light in his spiritual form, but it's the image of him as he appeared to Roc as the half man, half beast that people most remember.

If Roc was open to sharing his experiences and interactions with the nature spirits, he was much more discreet and veiled when it came to his studies. Hermetic magic is a particular approach to the subtle worlds with a lineage dating back several hundreds of years within the Western magical tradition to fifteenth-century Italy (though the roots of many of its concepts and practices go back much, much further even than that). Roc's work as a protector of Findhorn was a specific application of his role and work as a protector in a much larger sense. He said once to me that he had been given a specific charge to deal with the messes that people could create in the etheric or subtle body of Britain by working with subtle energies in ignorant and untutored—or even unscrupulous—ways. Part of this work involved occasionally travelling about Scotland and England to various natural power points to cleanse them of unwanted psychic pollution and doing the same with the lines of subtle force, or 'ley lines', joining these centres together. Often Peter was the chauffeur for such expeditions, and on some occasions I went along to observe and to help.

But Roc's work was different from my own in this regard, and this created an interesting divide between us which he expressed as the separation between old and new ways of understanding and doing magic. More recently, a new and more ecological understanding of how to attune to and work with subtle energies has been emerging, one based on ideas of wholeness and interconnectedness. The focus now is on communication, imagination, mutual regard, and partnership, of which the collaboration between humans and nature spirits in creating the Findhorn garden is a good example. In this view, subtle energies are neither wholly in the environment as a natural force like electricity nor wholly in the individual as a power to be projected out to control the environment; rather they emerge through a collaborative relationship between them.

Much nonsense is written about magic and magicians, and the whole topic is surrounded with fantasy and glamour. Part of the problem is that magic is seen as a discipline set apart from the course of everyday life, and dealing with supernatural or extraordinary powers, rather than as a way of understanding and tapping into capacities and energies that are inherently part of everyday life and thus quite normal and natural. The danger comes when people gravitate to any study of spirituality, magic, or the use of subtle energies in order to be different and special rather than to become more fully part of everyday life and more capable of service. Roc was sensitive to this and went out of his way not to add to this problem by making himself, what he did, or magic in general seem special and out of the ordinary. But there is no question that in addition to his other gifts and his wholeness as a human being, he was also a true magician and servant of humanity.

NOTES

CHAPTER 6

1   Earth energies such as ley lines are natural paths
    which usually follow magnetic lines in a network all
    over the planet, linking natural power points. All
    living beings have a sensitivity to these paths—they
    form for example part of the navigation capacity of
    migratory birds and are also used by sea animals such
    as whales. The magnetic component is measurable
    and acts like a carrier wave for the non-physical ley
    energy. A convergence or concentrated criss-crossing
    of these lines carries a special intensity, is therefore
    considered a power point and many such places, for
    example Stonehenge, have become sacred to religious

use of some kind in history. Many great cathedrals in Europe are built on such convergences and hence are thought of as cosmic power points.

CHAPTER 10

1   The *Zelkova carpinifolia* is a tree with a relatively short trunk but many branches and twigs—it illustrates well the interconnectedness of all life for which the concept of the Tree of Life stands.

CHAPTER 15

1   Andrew Glazewski was a Catholic priest and holistic lecturer who died in 1973.

CHAPTER 16

1   Reshad Feild is a Sufi lecturer and writer.

SOURCES AND ACKNOWLEDGMENTS

SOURCES

Chapters 1, 2, 3, 4 and 5 were edited from Roc's lecture 'The Elemental Kingdoms', previously published in *The Findhorn Garden* (Findhorn Trust 1970; Harper & Row 1975) and *The Findhorn Garden Story* (Findhorn Press 2008), © Findhorn Foundation 1975; in *The Magic Of Findhorn* (Harper & Row 1975; Souvenir Press 1975), © Paul Hawken 1975; in *The Kingdom Within* (Findhorn Press 1994), © Alex Walker and various contributors 1994; and as *The Elemental Kingdom* (Findhorn Foundation audio cassette 1975), © Findhorn Foundation 1975.

Chapter 6 was edited from an article by Brian Nobbs in the quarterly magazine *Network News* (Findhorn Foundation 2002); see also the author's website: www.briannobbs.com; © Brian Nobbs 2001.

Chapter 7 was retold from an account in 'The Wizard Meets The Elf-King', Chapter 8 in *The Magic Of Findhorn* by Paul Hawken (Harper & Row 1975; Souvenir Press 1975); © Paul Hawken 1975.

Chapter 8 was edited from 'ROC's Talk to the Gardeners', a private paper distributed at Findhorn, 1974.

Chapter 9 was edited from 'Linking Up Of Gardens', a private paper distributed at Findhorn, 1969.

Chapters 10, 11, 12 and 19 were edited from Roc's lecture 'Conversations With Pan', presented at the Findhorn conference, Man, Nature and The New Age in 1974, and later published in the magazine *One Earth 2* (Findhorn Foundation 1976) and as an audio cassette, also titled *Conversations With Pan* (Findhorn Foundation 1975).

Chapter 13 was edited from *The Findhorn Garden* (Findhorn Trust 1970; Harper & Row 1975), new edition *The Findhorn Garden Story* (Findhorn Press 2008); © Findhorn Foundation 1975.

Chapters 15, 16, 17 and 18 were edited from 'Elementals of Earth, Air, Water and Fire', a lecture Roc gave at the Widening Horizons conference at Attingham Park, England, New Year 1970–71.

RECOMMENDED READING

Crombie, R. Ogilvie, *Encounters with Pan and the Elemental Kingdoms* (CD), Findhorn Press, Forres/Scotland, 2010

Findhorn Community, *The Findhorn Garden Story*, Findhorn Press, Forres/Scotland, 2008

Hawken , Paul, *The Magic Of Findhorn: The extraordinary community where man co-operates ith plants, where people are transformed, where nothing is impossible and legends are reborn*, Souvenir Press, London, 1975

Maclean, Dorothy, *To Hear the Angels Sing: An odyssey of co-creation with the devic kingdom*, Lorian Press, Issaquah/ USA, 2008

Maclean, Dorothy, *Seeds of Inspiration: Deva flower messages*,
    Lorian Press, Issaquah/USA, 2004
Ripley, Frances, *Visions Unseen: Aspects of the natural realm*,
    Findhorn Press, Forres/Scotland, 2007

FINDHORN PRESS

Life-Changing Books

Learn more about us and our books at
www.findhornpress.com

For information on the Findhorn Foundation:
www.findhorn.org